BATTLE

OF THE

GODS

LUIS MARRERO

ISBN 979-8-88540-840-0 (paperback)
ISBN 979-8-88540-841-7 (digital)

Christian Faith Publishing
832 Park Avenue
Meadville, PA 16335
www.christianfaithpublishing.com

Printed in the United States of America

I dedicate this book first and foremost to the Heavenly Father, who granted me the vision to put together this work of art. Secondly, I dedicate it to my beloved mother Haydee Villafane, who I believe is sitting beside the Creator, smiling down upon me knowing that I changed my life for the better. I love you, Mami, and can't wait until the day that I get to see you again. For the time being, continue to shed those blessing on me from up above please. And lastly, but definitely not least, to my three beautiful sons, Luis, Jalen, and Lorenzo. I always told you guys that you can do whatever you desire in your hearts, just as long as you put in the time, effort, hard work, and dedication. I hope that this book inspires you all in the same way that unknowingly you guys helped inspire me to keep going at this so that I may be able to provide you all with a better life. I love you all, Dad.

Contents

CHAPTER 1

In the beginning God created the heavens and the earth. Now the earth was formless and empty, darkness was over the surface of the deep, and the Spirit of God was hovering over the waters. And God said, "Let there be light," and there was light. God saw that the light was good, and he separated the light from the darkness. God called the light "day," and the darkness he called "night." And there was evening, and there was morning—the first day. (Gen. 1:1–5)

"So what do you think of this place?"

"It's beautiful, Father," said Adam as he admired the serene atmosphere.

"It's like our very own paradise," replied Eve shortly after.

Both were mesmerized as they strolled through the plush grassy meadows, taking in the sounds of the birds chirping through the air, the flow of the waters as they cascaded off the rocks downstream, and even the buzzing of honeybees as they went from flower to flower pollinating each one.

"All of this, including the two of you I have created in my image, is for you to do as you please, wish, and desire. The only thing that I ask of you both is that you stay away from the trees of life and knowledge," spoke the Father. "Do I make myself clear of this?"

Adam and Eve looked at one another prior to looking to the Father, and both replied, "Yes, we understand."

"Eve, Eve, where are you?" Adam shouted as he ran through the forest hastily. "Eve!" He passed by a pair of baby fawns, which were grazing on some luscious grass. His screams caught the attention of the deers, which sent them scurrying in the opposite direction of him.

"I'm over here," she shouted upon hearing his calls. He turned to see her casually swimming in the crystal-clear pond.

"How's the water feel today?" he asked, hearing the edge, preparing to enter the waters with her.

"It's just the perfect temperature," she replied as she pressed her hand together and pushed forward, sending a splash of water onto him. This caused Adam to dive into the waters, where they swam and frolicked for a while.

"Why do you think that the Lord doesn't want us touching the trees of life and knowledge?" Eve asked as they were exiting out of the waters.

"I do not know, Eve, but the Father says that we shouldn't, and therefore we must oblige to his commands," Adam stated as he laid beside her on the grass to dry off with the help from the rays of the sun.

"Well, I think that we should find out for ourselves exactly what will happen if we have of it," she said as she got up and sprinted toward the center of the garden—the garden of Eden. Upon hearing her words and footsteps, Adam opened up his eyes and noticed that she was no longer by his side. He quickly rose up onto his own two feet and gave chase after her. Being much faster than her, he closed the gap easily between the two of them. But the distance to the center of the garden was not that far off from the pond. And therefore, she made it to the trees just before he could reach out to stop her.

The trees were magnificent—standing strongly rooted into the ground and rising well above everything else. They were high above into the skies. The way in which the light illuminated through their branches gave them a radiant aura, which made them look mighty and angelic in comparison to the rest of the trees nearby.

"Eve, don't," Adam pleaded with her as she grasped out and pulled onto one of its fruit. "You know that our Father warned us to stay clear of this tree and its fruit."

But it was as if she were in a trance as she continued to bring the fruit even closer to her mouth.

"Don't do it, Eve," he begged of her once more with the sounds of desperation waning faintly into the breeze as she slowly bit into the forbidden fruit. Its juices slowly seeped from the sides of her mouth from how soft and ripe it was.

"You see, nothing to worry about, Adam," she replied as she wiped the droplets of fruit juice with her hand and then slurping them up before passing the fruit toward his direction. "Here, you must try some. It's delectable."

He hesitated for a moment as he continued watching her finish swallowing the remaining piece on her mouth. Noticing that nothing bad has occurred to her, he took ahold of the fruit and brought it ever so slowly toward his own mouth, closing his eyes first prior to partaking a bite of the fruit for himself. He let out a slight gasp as the sweet nectar landed upon his taste buds. Its savory flavor brought delight into him, leaving him in a euphoric state of bliss, which unbeknown to him enlightened his senses. Prior to opening his eyes, he saw a bright flash of light which had awakened his conscience.

> And the Lord God said, "The man has now become like one of us, knowing good and evil. He must not be allowed to reach the tree of Life and eat, and live forever." So the Lord God banished him from the Garden of Eden to work the ground from which he had been taken. (Gen. 3:22–23)

"Due to your disobedience, I banish you both from the garden of Eden and send you as outcast to live and roam among all of the beast of the land," declared the Almighty Father. "You will rule above all of the animals until your dying days, for from dust you were created and to dust you shall return. I grant you longevity in life, but only as long as you refrain from committing any more sin and stay true to my Word."

Adam and Eve went on to live in the wilderness. Toiling the soils of the earth day in and day out in order to produce harvest, fruits, and vegetables to consume and survive. Within due time, they began to procreate and populate the lands with their own seeds, starting with Cain and Abel.

"How can you sing praises to the Lord still with how he has treated us?" Eve asked Adam one day while hearing him chanting to the skies above as he worked the fields with their children.

"How can I not, my love?" was his reply. "After all, our punishment could've been far worse off if the Creator had wished." He secured the reins to the oxen for Cain to control. "But yet our Father found favor on us. Granted us mercy and blessed us with all these wonderful things to continue living and becoming a prosperous nation."

"Do you really consider this a great life!" Eve shouted at the top of her lungs, resentment resonating after each word as she spoke. "We must awaken each and every morning along with the sun, working until dusk comes. Tending to all of these livestock. Hunched over so much throughout the day, I look forward to nightfall so that my body could get rest. This is not a great life, Adam! A great life is what we had when we roamed freely through the garden of Eden, without any worries or stress in life. And definitely not any back pains or sore body parts come nightfall."

Adam looked upon his wife with saddened eyes. He felt immensely for her and for her pains. He too felt the aches of the day's labor and at times shedding blood, sweat, and tears, depending on what the task of the day was. But within himself, he knew that this was what was to be done because of the sin which they had committed while living in Eden.

"I am sorry, my love, and I promise to rub upon your aches tonight as we lay down to rest," he stated to her, trying to sound as comforting as he could while at the same time trying to put his soreness to the back of his mind so that he may continue with what he was doing.

CHAPTER 2

Then God said, "Let us make mankind in our image, in our likeness, so that they may rule over the fish in the sea and the birds in the sky, over the livestock and all the wild animals, and over all the creatures that move along the ground." So God created mankind and his own image, in the image of God he created them; male and female he created them. God bless them and said to them, "Be fruitful and increase in number; fill the Earth and subdue it. Rule over the fish in the sea, and the birds in the sky, and over every living creature that moves on the ground." (Gen. 1:26–28)

"Hello and welcome to The Joint dispensary, where we'll get you high but keep the prices low," Venus said, greeting the individual who had just entered into the store. This was her very own mantra, which she used to acknowledge all her customers.

"How may I be of service to you today and is there anything in particular that you like or seek?" she asked, her voice being soft-spoken and angelic like.

"I am just browsing at the moment, for it is my first time here." The man spoke with a raspy tone to his speech. "But so far, I do see something that I like," he said as he held his gaze on her eyes for a moment before beginning to glance upon all the beautiful flowers within the display racks. The comment brought a big smile on her face and a slight grin across his.

"Well, my name is Venus, Vee for short, and I'll be right here if you need any help," she said as she continued to attend to the customer in front of her.

"So this might sound corny, but your name is out of this world," the man said as he placed his items onto the counter. "I'm Mada, and it's a pleasure to meet you."

They now stood face-to-face from one another. The comment made her blush and flustered to the point where she was fumbling his merchandise.

"I'm so sorry. Will there be anything else for you?" she asked as she bent over to pick up what she had dropped and placed it into the brown paper bag.

"No, I think that'll be all for today. Unless I can get your phone number or some way to contact you?" he asked.

"Woooh, Wilber, don't you think that you're moving too fast?" she retorted back in a playful manner. "We just met, but you know where to find me, and the store's phone number is on your receipt."

"Touché, that's fair enough," Mada said as he grabbed his package of goodies and headed toward the door.

"Oh, one last thing, Mada," Vee said right before he exited. "That was a corny line you used, but I like your confidence. See you around, I hope."

"Then God said, let the lands produce vegetation: plants bearing seeds according to their kind, and God saw that it was good," Mada recited the shortened version of Genesis 1:11–12 as he took a nice long drag of his blunt, holding in the smoke before releasing what seemed to be a cloud from his lungs.

This was one of his favorite passages of the Bible. He'd tell people, "If God opposed marijuana, why would he speak about it in the very first page of the good book? And why would he name it after his two beloved ladies, Mary of Magdalene and Mother Mary?"

Laying on his couch and listening to some Bob Marley, he replayed his interactions between Venus and himself over and over as he continued to puff away at his cigar filled of ganja.

"See you around, I hope. See you around, I hope," her voice echoed in his mind as his eyes closed and he drifted off to sleep.

Little did she know that he lived off hope, as well as faith and the grandest of all emotions, LOVE…

He woke up feeling well rested and rejuvenated. It was very seldom that Mada would get a full night of sleep without being awakened by some sort of ill feeling or one of his many weird visions about life—both from the past and sometimes things unknown to him that would eventually take place later on in life. He never considered himself as a psychic or anything in retrospect, for his visions never really helped anyone. But within himself, he did kind of feel like Nostradamus being able to kind of predict what was to come in the near future.

Although, he was not able to hone in on it accurately. This was something which he kept to himself and hardly ever shared with anyone. What got it tiresome to him was hearing that he was crazy, insane, hallucinating, or just had a wild and vivid imagination, especially when that doubt would come from those who were closest to him. He felt that if his very own family could ridicule him, what would the rest of the world think of him considering that he was a stranger? Not to mention the month he had to endure in the state mental institution as a teenager when he had the reoccurring dream of planes crashing into multiple buildings prior to 9/11 and the attack of the twin towers in New York. That was the first and last time he made a big issue about his visions. What he feared were the consequences that would come back on him. From that day forward, he bottled his visions within himself. But something, or someone, would always leave him feeling guilty about this.

"Hello, thank you for calling The Joint. Can you please hold?" Venus spoke into the phone.

"Sure, but only if I must," replied the man on the other end. By the man's accent and tone of voice, she kind of knew already who it was before placing the phone back on the receiver and attending to the multiple customers in the store. Freebie Fridays was always one of the busiest days of the week for multiple reasons. One, it was the beginning of the weekend. Two, it was payday. And of course, reason number three, the free merchandise that each and every customer received depending on how much their total purchase amount was.

It helped even more that they could make many purchases throughout the day and still receive some type of item for free varying from accessories to edibles, ointments, and tinctures, or even some pre-rolled joints.

"Hey there, cornball, sorry for the wait. How may I be of service to you today?" she spoke into the receiver after getting doing spare time in-between customers.

Mada chuckled. "Cornball, huh? Is that the politest way that you speak to all your customers?"

"Only the ones who leave a lasting impression," she responded in return with a feeling of warmth rushing throughout her body from her brazen reply.

Typically, Venus was timid and shy, always keeping to herself and only bring courtesy to her customers because the job entailed her to have to interact with people.

"So I made an impression on you, huh? Let me say that the feelings are mutual, but you should already know this from the way which I couldn't take my eyes of you the other day."

His reply brought back flashbacks into her mind of how things had played out among them.

"But anyways, I was wondering what time you work until today, if you had any prior plans, and if you'd like to hopefully hang out and get better acquainted with this cheesy cornball?" he asked.

The way with which he spoke into the phone, how he was okay to make fun of himself, and the way with which he said *hopefully* made her melt on the other end of the line.

"Six o'clock," she said after a brief moment of hesitation.

"And nothing too important that I couldn't put off until later on in the weekend. But hanging out with you depends on what all you have in mind," she said half as a statement and half as a question.

"Well, how about I swing by the store before you close? I need to restock up on my goodies and supplies anyway. As to what we can get into, we can decide on that together. After all, I'm still learning this town," Mada said. "See you later, I hope."

"I hope so too," Venus replied before hanging the phone up.

CHAPTER 3

Then the Lord said to Cain, "Why are you so angry? Why is your face downcast? If you do what is right, will you not be accepted? But if you do not do what is right, sin is crouching at your door; it desires to have you, but you must rule over it." Now Cain said to his brother Abel, "Let's go out to the field." While they were in the field, Cain attacked his brother Abel and killed him. Then the Lord said to Cain, "Where is your brother Abel?" "I don't know," he replied. "Am I my brother's keeper?" (Gen. 4:6–9)

"Nooo, oh, my God, no," Adam wailed as he held Abel in his arms. "How could you allow for this to happen, Father God?" He looked up to the heavens hoping for an answer. "He was a good boy. He did no wrong or harm." He cradled the lifeless body of his son on his arms, rocking from side to side in disbelief.

"So how much favor do you think that the Creator still has in us? If he were as just and merciful as you praise him to be, why would he permit such a thing, Adam?" Eve asked these questions with disgust in her words as they placed the final stones above the plot where they buried their son.

"Answer me, Adam!" she shouted. "Answer me now, dammit, or are you at a loss for words?" Eve cried out in vain, hate and anguish coming from her mouth as she beat against the ground with her hands balled into fist.

"I know that you're hurting, Eve, but please don't speak in that fashion. Don't take the Lord's name in vain."

"Don't you dare tell me how to act, Adam, nor how to speak. I am full of sorrow, and you dare try to control my emotions. Look at what's left of our son," she said, grasping handfuls of dirt and watching it slowly sift through the cracks of her fingers.

Adam bent down toward his wife and did the only thing that he could think of at the moment. He hugged her ever so tightly, held her close into his chest, and caressed her hair as she cried out. He held her this way until she fell asleep in his arms from exhaustion before carrying her into their encampment and laying her down to rest for the evening.

Nightfall was nearing, and Eve was still asleep. So Adam decided to go up onto the mountains to get some solace and pray. Upon ascending to the top, he built an altar, lit up some frankincense, and slaughtered an ewe as an offering to God. With his face bowed to the ground, he cried and prayed to the Almighty Creator.

"Heavenly Father, speak to me. Please accept this sacrifice and show me your face, Lord, for I am confused right now." As he prayed, the clouds in the skies thickened and amassed together above him. Sending fright through him upon noticing what was happening.

"Adam, do not be afraid, dismayed, or discouraged—for it is I, your Father," a voice spoke from up above him. "I am sorry for your grief, your loss, and the sorrows for which you now endure. Hear these words which I now speak to you, for they are a message to you, mankind, and all of humanity. Within you all now, your descendants, and all future generations to come, there is a conscience. A conscience which is aware of both good and evil, and this stems from the actions committed by Eve and yourself from eating of the tree of knowledge while in the garden. And as much as it hurts me to see sin and wickedness occur among the people whom I have created, it is something which I must allow to happen. This is called decision making, and it is up to you to teach one another how to make the right or wrong choices in life now. I still find great favor in you, Adam. Continue in your ways, and don't allow for yourself to be persuaded to do otherwise, son."

With that, the voice ceased, the clouds rolled back to their normal fashion, and Adam descended down the mountain to accompany Eve for a night of well-needed sleep.

Upon awakening the next morning, Adam told Eve of everything that had occurred the night before while he was on the mountaintop and the message which the Lord had sent.

"So you mean to tell me that our father is blaming us for the death of our son, Adam?" she asked. "Am I to accept that our son is no longer with us because we ate some fruit? Or accept that his death be placed on our hands although we had no part in it? That's blasphemy, and I cursed the Creator for the day with which he created us." Eve tore at the garments of clothing which covered her body.

"From this day forward, I wish to no longer speak of the Creator, hear of any messages which he has for us, nor shall I ever acknowledge him as my father, Adam," she belted out with much hostility and anger and then ran far from Adam for she wished to be alone.

"Who does he think he is? Who does he really think that he is?" she repeated over and over as if in a trance. With a wild look upon her face, she began to laugh in a sinister and hysterical way. A way in which she had never acted before, and at that moment, pure evil had entered into her mind and heart.

"I'll show him that he is not the only god," she said out loud. "I'll show him." She continued with the crazy laughter.

CHAPTER 4

Therefore, I urge you, brothers and sisters, in view of God's mercy, to offer you bodies as a living sacrifice, holy and pleasing to God—this is your true and proper worship. Do not conform to the pattern of this world, but be transformed by the renewing of your mind. Then you will be able to test and approve what God's will is—his good, pleasing and perfect will. (Rom. 12:1–2)

"Here I am, God, arms wide open," Mada sang along to the song playing on the radio station as he pulled into the parking lot for the dispensary.

"Pouring out my life gracefully broken," he continued as he exited from his 128i BMW convertible and headed toward door for the storefront. He was so caught up with the singing that he pulled on the door a little harder than expected, causing it to swing fully wide open. On the other end, Venus, having her hands full of merchandise, was walking backward toward the door to bump it open with her back. The timing couldn't have been any more perfect as she stumbled backward right into his arms. They were both caught off guard and taken aback from the freak incident of probabilities.

"Oh my g od, I'm so sorry," she said after collecting herself from being startled, but not yet turning around to notice whom she had bumped into.

"Don't be sorry. I'm not complaining at all one bit. But we might need to get you some hands with glue on them," he said as he retrieved the bag which had fallen out of her hands.

"Oh my god," she stated again upon hearing that voice. "Of all the people in this world, it had to be you, huh?"

"Well, hello to you too, Venus," Mada said as he handed over what she had dropped. "I'm not sure if that was destiny or out of luck, but either way, I'm thankful." He smiled.

"How about it was neither, and I just happened to not have a third hand," she said as she playfully brushed him out of the way with her shoulder to continue with what she was originally doing, delivering a curbside pickup. He watched her on amazement as she waltzed to the passenger side of the parked car of the customer. Her cut-off jean shorts was so form fitting that they almost seemed as if they were painted on.

He was mesmerized by the length of her hair which came down to her buttocks. This was something that he didn't see during their first interaction for she had had it up in a bun. And the way with which her caramelized skin glistened on the sun made him even more thankful to have chosen Florida as his new destination of residency.

"So, mister, what are the plans for tonight?" Venus asked as she turned the key to the second lock of the store door.

"Well, I'm not sure if you're hungry or not, but I was thinking that we could maybe grab a quick bite to eat and then maybe swing by Riverview Park and get acquainted as we sit by the waters," Mada said. "Plus I wanted to choose a location that wasn't secluded so that you'd feel safe around me. Considering that you don't know if I'm an axe murderer or not. Follow me or ride together?"

"Well, I take the bus because I don't drive, and I highly doubt that he'd be willing to follow you. So I'll hope that you left your axe at home," she said before inquiring which car was his.

"Oh, this is nice. We gotta ride with the top down please," she asked as they entered his vehicle. They decided on grabbing a few slices of pizza from Angelino's before jumping into US1 and heading toward Riverview and having their dinner down by the waters.

Ironically, NF's "Got You on My Mind" was now playing on the radio. They are on one of the many park benches, talked, and also watched a group of teenagers playing a game of volleyball. The weather was perfect as it was nearing the end of August, and the summertime breeze in the evenings was typically around the mid-seventies in temperature.

"So this might sound like a dumb question considering what you do for a living, but do you smoke buds?" Mada asked.

"Boy, is the pope Catholic, and do monkeys eat bananas? Of course I smoke, like an Indian as a matter of fact," Venus replied while tossing pieces of her pizza crust to the few birds that were near the tree besides them.

"Good. Then let's walk over to the dock pier and go burn one where we could get a little privacy from these people," he said, gathering up their trash and taking it to the garbage bin. They got high and talked for hours without a care in the world and forgetting about their phones. Sometimes their talks were being comical and whimsical and at other points a lot more serious and personal. He told her that he was from the country of Lebanon and he has lost his father at an early age due to his religious beliefs. The jihadist didn't take too kindly that his father was raising his family as Christians in a land among Muslims.

He also told her about his mother's passing in New York of a heart attack and how anxiety and depression led him to decide on getting away and relocating down to Florida for a fresh start in life away from the pains he endured. Venus, on the other hand, had opened up and told him how she also never knew who her father was, for she was the result of a rape, which her mother endured. But due to her religious beliefs, she had decided to keep the baby. Other topics varied from choice of music, bucket list wishes, and of course, they also spoke about good ole Mary Jane.

"Oh wow, I didn't realize how late it has gotten," Venus said, looking down and noticing what time it was on her phone. "Will you give me a ride home? The buses don't run at this time of hour."

"Sweetheart, even if they did, I wouldn't allow you to sit out here at this time of night all by yourself waiting for a bus, no matter how nice of a town this is. Where do you live?" Mada asked.

"Wabasso," she said after a brief pause.

Somewhat ashamed and embarrassed because she didn't live in the best of places. "Okay, I know where that's at. I drive pass there often. Both to go toward my place in VLE and also when I come down toward the river and beach," he said. "I can't believe that we only live about ten minutes from one another." Mada passed the blunt in her direction as he drove her home. It was the perfect smoke ride for the blunt was just ending as he pulled up beside her place.

"Well, I hope to see you again. I had a really great time tonight," Venus said as she was getting ready to exit his car.

"Don't you worry about that, sweetheart. I'm already looking forward to spending more time with you some day. And besides, I buy my buds from you."

"That's true," she said, letting out a laugh and feeling better hearing the words which he spoke.

"Oh, one more thing that I like to know about you, Venus. What's your last name?"

"De La Crux, why?"

"No real reason, just curiosity, that's all," he said.

"Oh, okay, and you?" Venus asked, figuring that if he knew her full name that she should know how as well.

"DeSol," Mada replied.

"All right, well, thanks again for everything, and have a good night, Mr. DeSol."

"It was my pleasure, Venus. Good night to you as well."

CHAPTER 5

When human beings began to increase in numbers on the earth and daughters were both to them, the find of God saw that the daughters of humans were beautiful, and they married any of them they chose. Then the Lord said, "My spirit will not contend with humans forget, for they are mortal, their days will be 120 years." The Nephelim were on the earth in those days—and also afterwards—when the songs of God went to the daughters of humans and had children by them. They were the heroes of old, men of renown. The Lord saw how great the wickedness of the human race had become on the earth, and that every inclination of the thoughts of the human heart was only evil all the time. The Lord regretted that he had made human beings on the earth, and his heart was deeply troubled. So the Lord said, "I will wipe from the earth the human race I have created—and with them the animals, the birds, and the creatures that move along the ground—for I regret that I have made them." But Noah found favor on the eyes of the Lord. (Gen. 6:1–8)

A great number of years had come and gone among the ground of the earth, and mankind had now started to become a small civilized society within the lands. There were people who had become herders of livestock, and others who made tools out of bronze and metals. While yet some made musical instruments out of string and pipes. Even Adam and Eve had another child within those years whom they had named Seth. And he too went on to grow old and have a son of his own which he had named Enoch.

"Adam, Adam," Eve repeated his name as she roused at his arm, shaking him lightly but also with enough strength that he would get up. After a few attempts, he shifted over and let out a light grunt.

"Adam, are you awake?" she asked. "There something that I want to dish to you about."

Upon opening his eyes some and noticing that it was still in the midst of nightfall, he stammered, "Can it wait until the morning, my love?"

"No, it can't, Adam. This is something that I've been holding in within myself for quite some time now, and I need to get it off my chest," she said.

Sensing that this was something which she wasn't going to put off any longer, he reluctantly awakened and propped himself up to give her his attention. "What is it, Eve?" he questioned her upon getting comfortable.

"Adam, we are not getting up there in age, and I feel that our days are now numbered," she whispered as if not wanting anyone what to hear the word which she spoke.

"Yes, you may be right, Eve, but did you really want me up to talk about how old we're getting?" he asked, the sound of annoyance coming from his mouth for being awakened to talk about age.

"Well, yes and no, Adam, but there also more to it. Just please keep quiet and listen to what I have to say without any interruptions please," Eve said, more as a demand and not a plea.

"Okay, fair enough, go on so that I may get some more rest once you're done doing what you feel is so important at this time of night, Eve."

"I don't want to die, Adam, nor do I want you to perish," she spoke.

He went to open his mouth and tried to say something when she quickly raised her hand and put a finger over his mouth. "Ahhh, I told you no interruptions, right?"

He nodded his head in agreement and allowed her to continue.

"I looked around on the ground and I noticed more and more burial sites of those deceased and now going from the earth. Beginning with our son Abel, remember?" she questioned.

To which once more he nodded his head but kept silent.

"I don't want that to be us, Adam, no matter what the Creator said about returning to the dust from which we had originally come from."

This was actually the first time which she has mentioned it, acknowledging the Father since the day which she had cursed his name many years ago

"So what are you getting at with this?" Adam quickly blurted out hastily out of fear of being quieted again.

"What I am getting at of this, Adam? Do you remember when we lived among him in the garden?" she asked, not wanting to speak of the Lord's name once more. Again, Adam nodded his head but remained silent, not knowing where all this was leading to but at the same time not wanting to interrupt as much as he needed to.

"There were two trees, Adam. The one which he placed cherubim and that flashing sword to protect and keep others away from it. At that time in life, there was nobody on this earth but us, Adam. He put those angels by that tree to keep *us* away from it. Did you not ever wonder why? Why he would go to such great lengths as to keep us away from that tree?" The way which she spoke did not sound like the Eve which he knew. Nor did the look on her eyes resemble the wife whom he had loved for hundreds of years. They were fully black in color, but he could not see this very well due to the full lighting and how dark it was outside.

"I have wondered this many nights over within myself since the moment we were removed from the garden, Adam, and this is what I've come up with. That tree was called the tree of life. That tree would give us the ability to become like him. To become a god and live forever. We would have eternal life and be immortal," Eve spoke before letting out a cry of laughter and a sinister grin appearing across her face.

At that very moment, Adam recalled the words which the Father had spoken to him many years ago while on the mountaintops when he prayed for Abel. *I still find great favor in you, Adam. Continue in your ways and do not allow for yourself to be persuaded to do otherwise.*

"Eve, please lie down with me and get some rest, my love," Adam spoke, not wanting to hear any more of what she was saying but also because he was somewhat afraid of her at the moment knowing that something evil was within her and wanting to pray to the Heavenly Father to send his Spirit so that it may touch her wicked and cold heart. That night, he solemnly cried himself to sleep as he spoke to the Creator within himself asking for forgiveness. Both for Eve and for himself. Little did he know this would be his last prayers. He passed away in his sleep, altogether living 930 years.

CHAPTER 6

It is not to angels that he has subjected the world to come about which we are speaking. but there is a place where someone has testified: What is mankind that you are mindful of them, a son of man that you care for him." You made them a little lower than the angels; you crowned them with glory and honor, and put everything under their feet. (Heb. 2:5–8)

"Thank you for saying yes and coming along with us to service, Mada. It really means a lot to me whether you know it or not. Mother and I have by coming to this church since before I was even born," Venus said in a way that left him with a perplexed look on his face.

Sensing his confusion, she decided to clarify what she had said. "Okay, so to remember what I told you the other day about my mother and how I came to be conceived, well, it was Reverend Bishop McNeilson who saw my mother lying face down on the canal. All bloodied and left to die. Ironically, the only reason that he had even pulled over on the side of the darkened and desolate road was because he had noticed my mother's gold-tone stilettos and intended to give them to his wife. The evil men who violated my mother were too careless to have noticed her shoes fall before tossing her restless body over the side of the road. But it was that simple act which allowed for my mother to be rescued and saved from death. What they didn't know right then at that very moment was that they saved two lives."

Mada looked at her with pain and sorrow in his eyes. For although she had mentioned about her mother's rape, she had not gone this far into detail about it.

"I'm sorry, Venus, both for you and also for your mother who had to suffer that type of cruel torture," he spoke.

"It's okay. I have come to terms of acceptance and also forgiveness for what those men did. The only thing that bothers me is that they have never been caught and continue to live life freely unpunished for their crime. I mean, who knows if they've ever done something like that again. That just means more helpless victims."

The words hit closer to home for Mada, knowing how he would have his visions and always feel guilty about not being able to help.

"Anyways, that's enough with the dad stories. The service is about to begin, and I like to introduce you to my mother beforehand," Venus said as she grabbed him by the hand and led him to the entrance of the church.

The New Voice of God Church was unlike any other church that Mada had been to, both there and back in his home country. There were people of all races and ages among the congregation. He saw blacks, white, Spanish, and even Asians. The way in which they all mingled together, smiling with one another, hugging each other, and talking with each other made it feel like a true place of worship. You could sense the love among everybody, and although this was only his first time there, he could see that they viewed each other as one big family. This was something that he could get used to considering that he was all alone in this new state. Not to mention how festive the choir was and the giant projector screens on either side of the podium with the words to the songs so that everyone could sing along to. At the moment, they were playing "Break Every Chain" by Tasha Cobbs. This was actually one of his many favorites, and he found himself falling right in tune with everybody else.

"Let me introduce you to my mother Dolores," Venus said to him after they had excused themselves among the other patrons in the pew to get to their seats. She was the spitting image of her daughter. And besides a few lines starting to show around her eyes, one would've easily mistaken them as sisters if not for the formal introduction.

"So you're the Romeo that I've been hearing about lately," her mother said softly as to not be heard by many. "At least she has good taste." Dolores smiled as she extended her arm out to shake his hand.

As he reached his arm out to meet hers, he noticed the long deep scars which she had attained during that dreadful night with her assailants.

"Romeo, really?" Mada mused. "And here I was getting used to being her cornball, Ms. De La Crux."

"Boy, don't play yourself in the house of the Lord," Venus said jokingly as she nudged him on the side with her elbow.

Reverend McNeilson started his sermon, and it was about the LGBTQ community and the comparisons of gays in the Bible.

He was reciting from Genesis 19:4–5 and how all the men from Sodom had come to the house of Lot seeking out the two angels in order to have sex with them.

"I tell you now," the reverend spoke. "If we continue to be so accepting of the wickedness of the world today, we will become the next Sodom and Gomorrah. Pillars of salt all over earth."

The whole congregation broke out in Amens, hallelujahs, and lots of clapping.

He held nothing back and offered no apologies for his words, stating that this was a message from God himself and that there was no way in which he would misconstrue the words of the Lord. The service was coming to an end, and the choir immersed with "God Only knows" by King & Country.

After a few hugs and "God bless you" between the peoples, they headed toward the exit. "Mada, come here. I'd like to introduce you to the reverend if it's okay," Dolores spoke to him. They were formally introduced, and after the name exchange they shook hands. Reverend McNeilson held on to Mada's hand for quite some time with a tight firm grip before beginning to speak in tongues.

"My son, I'm not sure if you are aware of this, but you are a very special and important person in this world. The Lord has a very important purpose for you and has blessed you with a very special gift. One that you are very much aware of but not many people know. It is up to you to hone in on that gift and use it for how it was intended of you to do so. God bless you, and thank you for coming to the service," he said as he released Mada's hand.

"What was that all about?" Venus didn't hesitate to ask once they were outside and headed toward the parking lot. "That was the first time ever that I heard the reverend speaking in tongues, and like I said earlier, I've been coming to this church all of my life."

"I'm not sure, Vee, but after that, I need myself a nice blunt to recollect and ease my mind. Feel like joining me by the river after we drop your mother off?" he asked, having offered Dolores a ride so she wouldn't have to wait on the bus.

The one good thing about this town was that the rich millionaire folks funded the bus transportation for anyone and everyone no matter how often they used the bus. It was one of their ways to get a tax write-off at the end of the year. Another thing which they invested their money for the people was free city dumpsites in various locations. A person could literally take their old sofas, furniture, mowed grass, shrubbery, or anything else out that they didn't need anymore and it wouldn't cost them a dime. Only gas and time.

"It was a pleasure meeting you today, Dolores, and I look forward to seeing you around."

"Oh, I'm sure that you will, Romeo, as long as you don't lose interest in my baby girl," she said. "And thanks again for the ride."

"Maybe next time I can let my hair float on the air," she said this for it had started to drizzle when they mounted the car after the service.

"So are we still on for that blunt by the river?" Venus asked once her mother had exited the car.

"What was that line about the pope and the monkey," he replied, remembering how she had answered him before at the park. They both laughed at how he had phrased it.

"Only thing is that we'll just have to 'hot box' the whip, unless this rain subsides before we get there."

"Either way, we'll be on cloud nine in no time, flying high with the angels," Mada said.

"Dying of angels, mister. You care to enlighten me about that special gift of yours?" Hearing her inquire about this again let him know that she wasn't going to let it rest so easily. This bothered him. Some never looked at his visions as a gift but more so as a curse for he didn't know what they meant. But then the reverend's words caught to him at that very instant as he thought, *It's up to you to hone in on it and use it for what it was intended.*

The words echoed in his mind, causing him to daydream for a moment. Not even the cars beeping behind him could snap him out of it.

"Mada, the lights green," she said to him multiple times before the words registered in his head and he began to drive again.

The light now yellow from how long he had gotten stuck in his thoughts.

"Boy, are you okay? You just froze there for a minute."

"Yeah, I'm fine, Vee. Just need to get lifted already," he said, racing into the center console and puking out the pre-rolled blunt that he had in the wrap pack. "Spark this up for us please," he said as he pointed the blunt and lighter on her direction. "Go ahead and hit it a while before you pass it to me."

"You don't have to tell me twice. I intend to do so," Venus kidded with him.

"You know, I can't believe that your mother's name translates to 'pains of the cross,'" he spoke, trying to take the spotlight off himself and also change the topic some. "Especially knowing now what she has gone through in life."

"Well, would you like to know something else that you might find interesting or possibly amusing?" Venus offered, continuing with the topic of conversation going.

"My middle name is Milagros," she said.

"Miracle of the cross," Mada said, thankful for having taken Spanish for a year while in high school.

"Correct, and you are 'of the sun,' Mr. DeSol."

They both broke out in synchronized laughter from this exchange of information. There was something about her aura that made him feel so comfortable being around her. The mixture of her looks, their commonalities, and the good weed helped out some as well.

All this combined together made it easy for him to open up about his visions without any fear of being judged. As a matter of fact, he felt trusting in her, and also, a sense of ease had overcome him upon opening up to her.

"I think that the reverend was right today on saying that you're someone special and important, Mada. And I'm thankful that you've come into my life," she said, leaning over in her seat toward his direction and placing a kiss on his check. The gesture caught him off guard and left him sort of startled for a moment.

"Thank you for those kind words, Vee, for that kiss, and for allowing me into your life as well," he said in return to her. And just so you know, I look forward to the time which we spend together, getting to learn about one another. With time, I want to know everything there is about you while at the same time adding to your life."

"Wow, that was smooth, Romeo. My mother picked the right name for you," she said, holding his hand in hers.

"Now let's not make this a repeat like the other day. I have work tomorrow. And speaking about work, I never asked you what it is that you do for a living being able to afford a nice car and having a nice place to live in Vero Lake Estates?" Venus said.

"I'm an investor, and thankfully I was fortunate enough to invest in the correct stocks. But nowadays I'm more into cryptocurrencies," he said as he turned the car on and headed toward her place.

CHAPTER 7

Sing the children have flesh and blood, he too shared in their humanity so that by his death he might break the power of him who holds the power of death—that is, the devil—and free those who all their lives were held on slavery by their fear of death. For surely it is not the angels he held, but Abraham's descendants. (Heb. 2:14–16)

Neigh, neigh, neigh. Eve awakened to the call of one of their ewes. Upon stepping outside, she noticed that the animal was laid on the ground suffering from labor pains. It groaned in a song as it writhed back and forth as it tried to pass the baby lamb. Knowing that labor with these animals was a two-person job, she ran back into their hut to get assistance from her husband.

"Adam, get up. One of the ewes is in labor with a lamb," she yelled frantically. "Adam, let's go. I need help." She went toward him to give him a stern shake. Upon feeling his arm, she felt a coldness which could only mean one thing. The call of the ewe became muted in comparison to the loud shriek which resonated from the bottom of her lungs.

"No, Adam, no. We were just talking to each other in the middle of the night. Wake up, please, wake up. You can't leave me like this, Adam, not now, not ever," Eve spoke to him as if he could hear her. As if her words would somehow wake him up from this eternal sleep.

"I told you that we needed to return to Eden," she yelled as she beat on his chest. "I told you, but you didn't want to listen to me.

You didn't want to hear me out, and now look at you, Adam." She cried aloud, completely forgetting about the ewe and the lamb.

"I will bring you back to life," she spoke to herself. "I vow to make it to that tree of life and bring you back into my life if it's the last thing I do, Adam. And then we'll live eternally together forever on this earth," she said. That cold stare with blackened eyes was across her face again.

She put together a sack of edible fruits, nuts, and grains, as well as some skins filled with water, and took off in the direction of the garden of Eden. As she passed the wailing ewe and noticed a spear not too far off from it, she gathered it, and without any hesitation, she thrusted it into the side of the ewe's neck. Immediately, it stopped crying and moving.

"How's that for a sacrifice?" she muttered before continuing on her journey into the wilderness with only one thought in mind.

The walk was a fast way off, for within the many years, they had ventured a good way from it, seeking out what else the barren lands had in store for them to discover when they were first cast out from the garden. She ignored the other people of the land as they tried speaking to her while passing by one another. No acknowledgment whatsoever, even when they passed within mere feet off each other. It was as if she had gone deaf and mute. But in reality, it was determination within herself that was driving her to get to where she wanted to be, without any distractions or deterrents to slow her down or possibly even put a halt to what her heart desired. Upon nightfall, she would rest propped up against a rock or tree. That blank look was still lingering on her face. And once the sun rose to illuminate her ways, she'd be right back to walking. In total, it had taken her three days to reach the outskirts of Eden.

From the distance, she was capable of seeing some of the rays of light radiating through the garden and shimmering off the streams of water which trickled alongside of her. For the first time since she had set out on her journey, she opened her mouth to speak.

"We made it, Adam. We made it, and we're almost there." She entered the garden and headed straight toward the center of it. With each step that she took nearer, the illuminescent lights became more brighter and also more entrancing. She was so close that she could now see the swaying swords and the two angels that were keeping guard and watching over the great tree.

"Halt, who goes there?" the angel to the left questioned upon sensing that someone was near.

"It is I, Eve," she answered as she stepped from beside the bush with which she had been crouched behind trying to seek refuge from their view.

"What brings you here, and what do you want?" the second angel spoke. "For you were banished from here."

"This is true, and you are right," Eve replied. "But there was no way which I could perish from this earth without having one last look out the tree's beauty." She explained to the angels what had happened to Adam and fearing that her time to leave the world was nearing as well.

"Does the Father know that you are here?" asked the first angel.

To which Eve replied,"For he not know everything being the Creator of all on these lands?" Her response was that perfect one—it had eased both of the angels to a point that they weren't so defensive anymore.

"Now let me ask you guys a question. Aren't you jealous or envious of the other angels who roam the lands among mankind? Partaking of the gorgeous daughters of us humans and fulfilling their desires with woman," she said with a sultry tone to her voice.

"Why should we feel any ill will toward our brethren?" the angel nearest to her asked.

"I don't know, just curiosity," Eve responded while at the same time removing the skins of water and the sacks of her food and placing them onto the ground. "I kind of just figured that you two would want to enjoy some of that fun rather than have to stand guard among a tree all days of your lives."

"Well, if you must know, until today, we have never seen a woman but only heard of them. So how could we desire what we do not know of?" the angel asked as he gazed upon Eve, taking in her looks and also acknowledging the differences between her body and theirs. And although she was well of on number of years on earth, she still held her beauty. But also unbeknown to them was that upon entering into the garden, her looks were bestowed back upon her as to the day when the Heavenly Father had first created her. For in the garden, nothing ever withered or got old. Eve, sensing that the seed of desire was now implanted into their conscience, slowly disrobed. Piece by piece, she removed every bit of garment of clothing which she had on until she stood there in front of the angels fully naked and also fully aware that the plan which she had concocted within her mind was working accordingly.

She pulled back her long brownish-blond hair that was covering her breast and allowed for herself to be fully exposed to the angels. Exposed in the same way which she had become when she first partook of the fruit from the tree of knowledge, only this time she did not feel naked or shame like she did before.

"This is for you, Adam," she shouted before saying to the angels, "come and enter me so that you may know what it feels like to become one with the flesh."

Then she laid down on the ground and waited in all of her glory. The angels becoming fully aware of desire now could no longer contain themselves as they had now become aroused. They stepped away from the tree, put down their swords, and took off their armor plates. She allowed for them to have their way with her and waited patiently for the right opportunity to continue with the plan which she had derived within her head days ago when she first took off toward the garden. She knew the she would only have one chance to be successful with her plans. Do anything wrong, and the outcome would be a quick and imminent death. She waited and watched the angels with the peripheral view of her eyes lying motionless. Upon seeing them both bending over to gather their armored chest plates, she felt that this was the right opportunity to continue as planned. Just like she had did with Adam many, many years ago, she arose and quickly sprinted toward the tree. The angels, being caught up in the process of getting dressed, stumbled among themselves as they tried to reach out for Eve and stop her from what she was trying to do.

Seeing that she was nearing the tree and sensing that it would be too late, the closest angel raised his sword backward in a throwing motion. Forcefully he thrusted his arm forward and released his sword. The throw was perfect, and the speed at which the sword traveled meant that it would reach its target with ease. Eve continued to run to the tree without one looking back, so she was unaware of the sudden death that was right behind her. She made it near the roots of the tree as the sword closed the gap between them within feet. Her arm extended outwardly so that she may be even closer to what could be the beginning of immortality if she were right about her presumptions. Simultaneously, she felt the piercing of the swords point as it began to penetrate through her back while at the same time grasping onto one of the branches from the tree, its leaves gliding in between her fingers. Immediately a blinding bright flash occurred, followed by an enormous deafening bang which shook the realms of the earth like something never felt before. The two angels were thrown back onto the grounds forcefully from the impact of the bang.

Once they had regained their senses and were able to see, they noticed that the Almighty Creator was now standing there in front of them.

"What wickedness have you two done?" he spoke. "And how could you allow for this to happen?" Anger was coming from his words.

They both became full of fear at seeing how angry the Father had become. Then the angel with his sword quickly turned it upon himself and thrusted it through his own stomach, taking his life. The other angel bowed to the ground and began sobbing while asking for forgiveness.

"A sin as severe as this does not merit forgiveness," the Creator spoke, preparing to strike him dead where he was. As the Lord raised his hand to cast judgment upon the angel, a sword came flying beside him, which found placement around the angels neck, decapitating him instantly.

"I believe this belongs to you," the Creator heard a voice say followed by sinister laughter. He turned around to see Eve standing beside the tree of life.

"Hello, Father, did you miss me?" she said with a sly smile on her face.

CHAPTER 8

Obadiah' the vision of Obadiah. This is what the Sovereign Lord says about Edom—we have heard a message from the Lord: an envoy was sent to the nations to say, "Rise, let us go against her for battle."

"Solve the mystery about the girl, Mada. The answer lies within the girl."

"What girl, Papa? I can't do it on my own," he questioned his father in his dream, the same way it has happened every time he had this dream when he was a child. He never got any further than this point before waking up in cold sweats.

"You have help now," his father said before vanishing.

This last line was something new to a reoccurring dream which he had had dozens of times since his teenage years. He woke up confused and perplexed about this new added line. More questions were added to the ones which he already had previously.

Is the girl Venus? Or possibly Dolores and the ordeal which she suffered? And who is my help, Papa? he questioned his thoughts. He turned over to glance at the clock and saw what time it was. It was still dark outside, 5:40 a.m.

"Looks like another early day for me," he spoke to himself knowing that he would not be able to get any more rest after having this vision, not even the time when he would awaken earlier than this. He could not find it within himself to fall back to sleep. He rustled himself out of his enormous king-size bed and headed toward the kitchen to fix himself a quick bowl of cereal, along with two hard boiled eggs and a glass of orange juice before jumping in the shower and then heading out toward the gym. He enjoyed the gym at this time of day for it wasn't that crowded, common for him to typically not have to wait for usage of any of the equipment. Plus, it also gave him the rest of the day to go about as to however he pleased. Today he had decided that he would do some ocean fishing off the pier down by the inlet. He rang out to Venus as he had stored his rods and tackled into the trunk of his car.

"Hey, sweetheart, how are you and what are you up to at the moment?"

She informed him that she was en route to the bus stop to wait as she had to open the store by 10 a.m.

"All right, well, don't jump on the bus, and wait for me there," he said. "I'm headed in that direction as we speak. I'll give you a ride to work."

As they smoked a blunt, he filled her in about his dream and also the new line.

"What do you think it means?" Venus asked as he was turning into the shopping place to where the dispensary was.

"I'm not sure. Here I was hoping that you knew since my father mentioned that I have help now." He smiled at her trying to make light of the matter.

"Well, I wish I had the answer for you, Mada, but I'm just as dumfounded by this," Venus said truthfully for this was the first time that he had mentioned this vision to her. Being high this early in the morning wasn't helping out at all either.

"I'll tell you what, though. I'll give it some thought today while I'm stuck here for the next eight hours. For now, though, I must get up in here and start running shop," she said, noticing that there were a few customers already sitting in their cars waiting patiently for the door to open so they too may get their morning wake and bake.

"You have yourself a wonderful day fishing, Mada. The weather is perfect for it. Don't beat yourself to death about it, and also don't get pulled in the waters by a shark," she said, trying to help ease his mind some before having to leave his side. In what now had become tradition to her, she leaned over and gave him a kiss on the cheek. As always, the gesture brought a smile upon his face.

"Vee," he slightly yelled her name while lowering the passenger side window to get her attention.

"Yes," she asked while running around to acknowledge him.

"Would you like to do something different and exciting with me later on after work?" he asked.

"Sure, Mada," she answered without knowing or asking what it might be.

Mada jumped onto A1A North of 510 and ventured off onto what he was hoping to be the beginning of a good, fun-filled day in comparison to how it had begun in the morning. He paid his $4 passing fee and entered into the parking area of the Sebastian inlet. This was one of many inlets scattered among the state of Florida. But from what information he had gathered from many of the locals, it was one of the more renounced ones when it came to fishing, not to mention that it happened to be the closest one to him in distance from his house. The second nearest one was the "Jetty" in Fort Pierce. But he was not too fond of it, for he happened to catch many "rock fish." And by rock fish he really meant that he would snag up on the rocks all the time and at times, spending most of the day restringing his line with hooks and weights rather than actually doing any fishing at all. Fishing had become one of his favorite hobbies to do ever since he was a young boy living in New York. This was a pastime of his that allowed for him to occupy his mind and thoughts, allowing for him to get some temporary escape from his visions. And even if he would go home empty-handed, he would still find much joy out of being among the elements and being one with the universe. On those days, he would say to anyone who'd ask, "I fed the fish today."

Today wouldn't be one of those days he had told himself, recalling those times of yesteryears. To his amazement, the inlet was actually pretty full for how early in the day it was, not to mention that it was a day of the week. But then again, he was now living in what was widely world known as a retirement state. He enjoyed himself greatly and even took some time to do a little bit of swimming before wrapping things up and calling it a day. The best part of it being that he would not be going home empty-handed today, for he had caught a variety of fish ranging from sheepshead to snook and even a few ocean catfish, which was something that he was unaware which existed until coming down to Florida and catching them for himself. The sheephead blew his mind as well. For they had teeth which resembled those of human, which they used to break the shells of clams, mussels, and crabs. Loading away his belongings into the car, he smiled upon himself at the thought of knowing that he would be spending the evening with Venus.

He pulled into the storefront right as she was locking the place up, startling her as he pressed on the horn to get her attention. This made her jump, and the keys slipped out of her hands.

This time she was fast enough to reach out and catch them midair before they could fall to the ground.

"I see that you've been working on those reflexes," he said upon seeing what had occurred. She sucked her teeth at his comment as she walked toward his car and opened the passenger door.

"Ooh boy, you stink," she said, breathing in and inhaling the mixture of bait and dead fish. "I'm not sure what your plans are for us tonight, but I do sure hope that you plan on washing up first before we do anything."

The comment caused them both to laugh.

"Come here and give daddy a hug," Mada said playfully as he opened his arms wide on her direction.

"Ugh, ugh, you ain't touching me with those smelly hands, boy," she quipped. "The most that you'll get from me right now is an air five," she said, raising her hand and smacking them up toward him before leaning over and kissing his cheek. He asked her if she needed to stop by her house at all for anything and also if she was okay with going to his place real quick so that he may wash quick and change his clothes.

Not wanting to waste much time from the evening, she declined on swinging by her house and told him to just go to his place. They turned into VLE on 90th St and headed up to 104th Ct before he made a right into the road laid out with sand. This was something else that has blown his mind upon moving to Florida from up north. Many of the side streets were made of sand rather than the typical blacktop and asphalt, which he was used to from back home, and not to mention how bumpy they could get from needing to be smoothed out and graded every so often, depending on how much traffic had driven on them and also from the rains.

He pulled up into his driveway, and she took notice of his single-level ranch house with a two-car garage. From the look of the exterior, she could tell that it was a nice place and looked forward to seeing what the inside was like. Holding the front door open, he allowed her to enter first. They were now standing in his living room. And although it was clean and spacious, she immediately could tell that a man lived here.

"Nice place you have, but it could use a woman's touch," Venus said, noticing how plain and barren it was. It had just the bare necessities and not much more for home decor.

"Do you happen to be for hire?" Mada asked her before excusing himself to go wash up.

"I could lend a hand some time over the weekend when I'm off," she responded as he walked down the corridor to what she assumed was his bedroom and bathroom areas.

"Make yourself at home. The TV remote is on the sofa," he yelled from the back. Venus glanced around at the few family pictures which he had scattered throughout and noticed that most were of a woman that she presumed was his mother. There were two old Polaroids propped up against the TV of a man with a young boy no much older than two or three years in age. This she figured would have been Mada and his father. And based on the clothing which they were wearing, one could really see that the photos had been from his home country of Lebanon.

"That's my father and me," he spoke. His voice caught her off guard and caused her to jump some. "That was our last picture taken together, not long afterward from that photo being taken when they came and took his life." His voice trailed off as if he were remembering the day. It was something which she knew that would be almost impossible given his age in the picture.

"You were so young there," she said, stating the obvious. "You resembled him a lot, though, but how could you recall him so well?" she dared to ask.

"It's funny that you ask that, but also it is a question which I've had to answer before. Therefore, it isn't a difficult one to answer," he responded as he did the buttons to his shirt. "You see, my visions began of my father a couple years after his passing. I would tell my mother about my dreams that I would have," he went on telling her. "There were times when she would begin to cry from what I'd tell her, and at other times, she would get angry with me, questioning who had told me these things or put me on to tell her things. For there were a few instances when I had mentioned things that were from before I was even born." This last tidbit of information left her with her mouth ajar.

"I know that this is hard to digest, or maybe even hard to believe, but it is all true," Mada spoke, trying to reassure her that he wasn't crazy.

"I don't think that you're crazy or making any of this up," she said as if reading his mind. "I believed everything which you have told me since the very first conversation that we had when we meet at the dispensary."

"Thank you for this, Vee. It really means a lot to me. Now are you ready to have a great time tonight?" he asked, trying to change the topic at hand.

"Boy, of course I am," Venus said in agreement to his last question. "Shoot, I even passed on going home and washing up due to the excitement I have within myself wondering what you have in store for us."

"I know, I can smell you from all the way over here," Mada said jokingly. "But first and foremost, we have to get lifted before we go anywhere." He pulled out a small wooden box from underneath the sofa. Inside were the contents of the weed and supplies that he'd purchase from the dispensary.

"I agree with you," Venus said, sitting right beside him on the couch. Besides while at church or in his car, this was the first time that they were actually this close to one another without anything in between them.

"Thank you for having come into my life, Mada, and also for being so trusting in me," Venus said as she tried to hide the giddy feeling which she felt within herself. Mada went to the her, but before he could open his mouth to say anything, she kissed him on the lips. It caught him off guard, and this time, it was him who dropped the just finished rolled blunt onto his lap.

"Well, it looks like I'm beginning to rub off on you," Venus said, causing them both to break out in laughter. As they stayed in his living room smoking, he rolled a couple more blunts to save them for the evening.

"So where are we going and what are we doing?" she asked as he drove.

"It's a surprise, but I'll give you a hint and say that it's a safari," he replied. His answer left images of lions, elephants, and many other types of animals in her head. But with dusk nearing and knowing that the nearest zoo was in the next county over, his hint was as good as a $3 bill, useless. Having forgotten to grab themselves something to drink while at his place, they decided to stop by Ms. Marilyn's good store near her house before continuing on.

"Boy, am I glad that we stopped for this drink. My mouth was dryer than the Sahara desert," Venus said.

"Tell me about it. Mine was too," he agreed with her as he slipped on his orange juice and put the car in reverse, not noticing the older gentleman going behind him on bike.

"Hey, hey," the man yelled out with enough warning to allow for Mada to slam on the brakes and missing the guy. But for some reason, the man found it necessary to put his leg out and kick at the car. This caused Mada to exit the vehicle with a little bit of hostility.

"What's your problem, man? Was that really necessary?" Mada asked the older gentleman who had by now reached into his pants pocket and pulled out a switchblade.

"Whatcha wanna do, young blood?" the old man asked, his blade glinting add the light hit it. At that very moment, Mada became a little dizzy and lightheaded. This he thought was from being thirsty and also from how fast he had moved to get out of the car.

"Mada, don't. Just get back into the car," Venus said, seeing the knife in the old man's hand. Her voice brought him back to reality. Not wanting to risk being hurt and also ruining the night with

Venus, he slowly and hesitantly got back into the car and locked the doors. The older man pocketed his knife and rode off through the rent side street.

"That was crazy," Venus said when things had settled. "We should call the cops."

"No, it's okay, Vee. Nobody was hurt, and I don't want to lose more time right now having to wait on a cop and manning a report. Let's just go enjoy our night," he said.

"Did that man look familiar to you at all?" he questioned her since the altercation had occurred in the vicinity of Wabasso.

"No, I've never seen him before, but then again, I couldn't get a good look of him either," she told him, not wanting to have gotten out of the car. They made it to Safari Joe's mini golf without speaking of what had transpired anymore, trying to make light of the situation and wanting to make the best of their time together.

"So this is the Safari, huh? I never knew that place was here," Venus spoke as he pulled into the parking lot and parked.

"Wow, really? I'm beginning to question which one of us is the local, and who isn't," he said. "You need to start getting out not, Vee."

"I will now, now that I have you in my life," she said.

They went on with the rest of their night having the time of their lives. Playing miniature golf while high was definitely an experience for the both of them. Venus even got a couple hold on one. While Mada on the other hand sent his ball flying off course and having to search for it on a bush for minutes from how hard he had hit the ball. This could've been from the aggression which he still had within himself from the ordeal earlier in the evening. All in all, it was the perfect night out. It was followed with some good soft-serve ice cream, and a nice blunt was waiting for the ride home. As they walked back to the car, they realized that the plastic was busted out from the left side of his lights. This happened to have been the side which the old man kicked out of anger earlier. There was some blood droplets around the broken shards of his taillight, and he could recall that the guy had been wearing flip-flops.

"We have to make a report now," Venus said, seeing the damage that was done to his car. "And with the blood, there's DNA that could possibly lead to a match on a suspect."

Mada asked to do so, but only when he had gotten her home with hopes that the neighborhood police might know whom the suspect was once he gave a good description of the individual. The police arrived to her place and took a full report of what had happened, as well as collecting a sample of the now dried-up blood on a Q-tip to run through their DNA database hoping to get a hit on a person that might be in their records. By the time everything was all said and done, it put the time at a little after eleven at night. Knowing that Venus had to work in the morning, he wished her a good night and headed home himself.

CHAPTER 9

So I say, walk by the Spirit, and you will not gratify the desires of the flesh. For the flesh desires what is contrary to the Spirit, and the Spirit what is contrary to the flesh. They are in conflict with each other, so that you are not to do whatever you want. But if you are led by the Spirit, you are not under the law. The acts of the flesh are obvious: sexual immortality, impurity and debauchery; Idolatry and witchcraft; hated, discord, jealousy, fits of rage, selfish ambition, dissensions, factions and envy; drunkenness, orgies, and the likes. I warn you, as I did before, that those who live like this will not inherit the kingdom of God. But the fruit of the Spirit is Love, Joy, peace, forbearance, kindness, goodness, faithfulness, gentleness and self control. Against such things there is no law. those who Benning to Christ Jesus have crucified the flesh with its passion and desires. Since we love by the Spirit, let us keep with the Spirit. Let us not become conceited, provoking and envying each other. (Gal. 5:16–26)

"Eve? Of course I should have known. How could you do such a thing?" the Creator asked.

"I could be asking you the same question," she replied. "How could you go on living with yourself knowing that you have allowed for your firstborn to die." Eve questioned God's authority. "Aren't you supposed to be merciful and forgiving?"

"I AM what you say I AM, Eve, and this is why I had allowed for the two of you to continue living when you first committed sin in this very garden so long ago," the Father said. "Me being the Creator, do you not believe that I could've taken your breath then just as easily as I had given it to you? Still, I had chosen to have mercy on you, even with your deceitful ways for I felt pity within myself. More so for Adam, who was led into wickedness through your sinful acts."

Hearing this and also hearing the name of her now deceased husband enraged Eve to the point that she threatened the Almighty Holy One and swore to avenge the death of Adam as she did a duck and roll toward the decapitated angel and picked up his sword. The Lord raised his arm, extending it outward. And like a magnet, the sword of the other dead angel came flying into his hand. Sparks flew, and a loud clang was heard as he deflected her blow before pushing her back a good distance from him with his other hand.

"Do not do this, Eve, for I do not wish to harm you."

"Ha, do you not think that I have become like you now, Father? A goddess," she spoke. "I knew that there was something special about the tree from the day that you banished us from Eden and decided to turn your back on us."

"My actions stemmed from the decisions which you made, Eve, and I will inflict my wrath once more if it is something that I must do again."

"Do not call me by that name, Father. From here on out, I will be known to the world as *Hades*," Eve said as she lunged in his direction with her sword outstretched in front of her. The Creator stepped to the side and once again gave her a push, which put some distance between the two of them. She turned around disgruntled from not being able to achieve a strike on the Lord.

"I will bring back Adam from the dead and change his name as well," she said, thinking to herself that this was a perfect way of showing disrespect to the one who has created them.

"His new name shall be Lucifer for he is made from the light," Eve said, referring to the bright flash that had occurred when she had reached the tree of life and touched it.

"I shall also lighten the color of his skin and change the size of his flesh, making him on the image to my liking and not yours," she added, wanting to show complete and total disobedience to the Creator. "I will contest every law that you make and enter into the minds of mankind so that they may oppose of goodness."

"My child, you go ahead and do what you deem is right in your eyes, although it is not, and I will show you that through faith and by my Spirit, this world I shall inherit. For the power of God will always overcome bad, just as the light of the heavens will always do away with darkness," the Father spoke with empathy in his words. "But as for you and all those who choose to follow you, Eve, I will cast down into the fiery pits of hell. To suffer in torment for all the wicked deeds for which they do while on the grounds of this earth which I have created." The Father then disappeared without a trace, leaving her there alone amid the center of the garden of Eden.

"And here I thought that you would put on a bigger fight than that," she yelled as she looked up to the skies upon noticing that there was nobody else around. Not even the two slain angels were there. For the Creator had taken them with him when he had dispersed from the earth back into the heavens. As she stood there gazing to the skies with her hands held outstretched above her, it started to drizzle. Little did she know that this drizzle was the beginning of a long rainfall. A rainfall that would wipe out almost all of humanity, including her body. For this was the start to the downpour of the great floods of which lasted forty days. The flood of the days of Noah which God has used to cleanse the world of all evil and impure people. From this day forward, the battle of the gods occurred through the forms of the spirits.

CHAPTER 10

That night God appeared to Solomon and said to him, "Ask for whatever you want me to give you." Solomon answered God, "you have shown great kindness to David my father and have made me King in his place. Now, Lord God, let your promise to my father David be confirmed, for you have made me King over a people who are as numerous as the dust of the earth. give me wisdom and knowledge, that I may lead this people, for who is able to govern this great people of yours?" God said to Solomon, "Since this is your heart's desire and you have not asked for wealth, possessions of honor, North for the death of your enemies, and since you have not asked for a long life but for wisdom acknowledge to govern my people over whom I have made you king, therefore wisdom and knowledge will be given you. And I will also give you wealth, possessions and honor, such as no king who was before you ever had and none after you will have. (2 Chron. 1:7–12)

"Hello and good morning, Mr. DeSol. This is Detective Randy Richards of the Indian County Sheriff's Office," the voice spoke into the phone. "I'd like to speak with you on person and get a little more information from you regarding the incident which occurred with you last night by the store. The sooner, the better."

Mada wondered to himself as to why there was a detective calling him when he had spoken with the sheriff's department when he had made the initial report. Either way, he agreed to meet up with Mr. Richards right away since he had the state thing to do so.

"Sure, where would you like me to come to?" he asked.

"How about at the door of the incident? I could be there in half hour if that works for you," the detective said.

"Sure, that's fine," Mada agreed once more while tossing the last bite of his egg sandwich into his mouth and washing it down with the rest of his milk before grabbing his keys and heading toward Ms. Marilyn's. He made it there with plenty of time to spare, which allowed for him to take a few tokes from the bowl. In good mind, there was no way that he would spend who knew how long out here with Detective Richards without being in his own element. He was just finishing up with the bowl and putting it away in the center console when he noticed the unmarked police cruiser turning into the store parking lot.

"Talk about perfect timing," he said to himself as he grabbed his cologne from the side of his door and exiting to meet up with the detective. After their introduction and some light pleasantries, the detective got right to work.

"From the sheriff's report, it says that you have a pretty vague description of the perpetrator. I was wondering if there was anything else since last night that you might've remembered?" he asked.

"I don't think so," Mada answered. "Like I told the other cop, it was becoming nightfall and everything happened so fast. Not to mention if I'm going to be honest, I was a little high at the moment."

"Yeah, sort of like you are right now," Mr. Richards said, noticing the redness in Mada's eyes and being able to lightly smell the aroma of freshly smoked marijuana through his cologne bath.

"You could tell, huh. That's why they made you a detective," Mada said, trying to get on his good side. "I do have my medical card if it means anything to you."

"I could care less about that, Mr. DeSol. What I have on my plate to deal with is a lot more serious than some weed," he said with straight seriousness in his voice. "So soon I'm gonna ask you if there anything at all that you can recall." He scanned the building's perimeter to check for any cameras. Unfortunately there weren't any that he could see.

"Besides the funky clown horn on the handlebars of his bike, there's not much that I can tell you, sir. The man was dressed in mostly dark clothes and wearing a hat as well. I would put his age at around the mid-fifties to early sixties with salt-and-pepper hair and beard. But besides that, there is nothing else which I could tell you," Mada said.

"All right, that's fair enough, Mr. DeSol. Now in case you were wondering why this case has been handed down to me, I'll enlighten you some," Detective Richards said. "We ran the cotton swabs of the blood from your car through forensic, and lo and behold, we were able to get a match from a cold case that happened almost thirty years ago around here. Sadly enough, though, that match could not provide us with a face or a name, which means that the perpetrator has never been arrested before and put into the DNA database. The department and I were really hoping the you could've been of a little more help." Detective Richards apologized if he had wasted both of their times by having Mada come out there so early to meet and talk.

"Sorry for not being able to provide you with anything else," he said, allowing for all the detective's information to digest.

"No worries about it, but just in case anything else might come to your mind later on the road, here's one of my cards. That's my direct number on the front," he said.

"Okay, sure enough, sir," Mada said, taking ahold of the business card and pocketing it. "Mr. Richards? May I ask you something before you go if you don't mind me asking? That cold case which you mentioned, what was the charge?"

"It was a brutal rape that we're also viewing as an attempted murder due to the severity of it all," was his reply. Upon hearing the words which came out of the detective's mouth, Mada had become lightheaded, knowing all too well that there was a big possibility that this cold case was in connection with Dolores and Venus. This could only mean that the man from last night was one of the individuals who had violated Dolores.

Right at that very moment, though, another question arose into his head. Could he have been standing face-to-face with the man who could possibly be Venus's father. The thought of it alone made him even more dizzy.

"Are you all right, Mr. DeSol?" the detective asked, noticing Mada's action.

"Yeah, yes, I'm okay. I just need to sit down for a minute," he said, entering into his car trip be in solitude and allowing for his senses and equilibrium to balance themselves out from the shock which he just received.

"What are the odds of this?" he asked himself still trying to make sense of the whole situation. Being near Venus's place, seeing how early it was, and knowing that she'd be home, he called her.

"Good morning, Vee. Can I come over?" he asked, letting her know that he was in the area.

"There's something that we need to talk about," he said to her as she entered his car. "But first I think that you should finish your test of this bowl," he said, passing it in her direction. He watched her as she smoked, giving him time to contemplate how he would break the news to her. After all, this was something huge that he did not know how she would take.

"What's on your mind, Mada?" she asked, seeing the look of concern on his face as she puffed on the bowl.

"Venus," he began. "What I have to tell you is something very serious, and I do not know how to even begin out where to start."

"Well, I'm a big girl. I can handle it," she said, not knowing the bombshell that was about to be dropped on her.

"All right, then, Vee. Here goes nothing," Mada said, taking in a deep breath to situate his thoughts and hoping to find the right words to explain it all to her.

"I just finished meeting up with a detective, Venus, and he told me something about the man from last night that I think you should know. And let me apologize ahead of time for wanting to tell you about it so quickly and so early, but it's something that I think you should really know."

"Boy, that's enough with the suspense," Venus said, unaware of the news she was able to receive. "Just spit it out."

"Very well, Vee. The detective informed me that he got a match from the blood. And that match was to a case from almost thirty years ago for a rape," he said. The words were like a smack to her face, and she dropped the bowl into her lap as she heard them, knowing very well what he was trying to tell her. Her eyes began to water, and her hands were now shaking from what she was just told. There was no more need for him to say anything. She put one and one together and knew exactly what this meant.

"I'm sorry, Vee," Mada said as he reached over to her to try and console her with a hug. She just cried out and shook on his arms as the news of it all sunk into her mind.

"How do I tell my mother?" was all that she could say as she looked him in the eyes.

"I don't know, but it's something that I'll leave up to you to decide when and how. But I could be there when you do so for some added moral support," he said, squeezing her a little tighter into his arms.

"Thank you for that," Venus said as she continued to sob in his arms. After the initial impact of it all was over, she decided that she would take the day off work knowing that she wouldn't be on the right state of mind to deal with anyone today. She also decided that she would tell her mother right away.

"After all, this was something that she has carried within herself for such a long time," Venus said to him.

"Yeah, I guess you're right, Vee. I'm ready whenever you are, soldier," he said, trying to build her courage for what was to come.

Dolores was just beginning to start her day. She had a fresh pot of coffee going and was adding sugar and creamer into her mug as they entered the house. This was Mada's first time being welcomed inside, and he looked around, taking all the place in. Instantly, he noticed that one of them was very much into Indians, by the dream catchers, figurines, and pictures throughout the place.

"I like this right here," he said, pointing to a frame of an older worn-down Indian chief with two wolves in the background. A saying on it read, "My body has been beaten down from my many years of battle, and one day it will exist no more. But my soul and my spirit will never cease but continue to roam the realms of this earth just as the spirits of our ancestors do."

"Yeah, that one is one of my favorites actually, and to think that I picked it up at a yard sale for only $1," Dolores spoke at his comment, letting it be known that it was she who was into the tribal decor.

"Do you know that this town was actually populated by Indians many, many years ago?" she said. "That was before the white man came from across the seas and took over. They even changed the name of the town, but at least they had the common decency to consider them in doing so." She continued to tell him that Wabasso was actually Ossabaw before. And how one could actually discover some old Indian artifacts if they chose to dig around in the grounds in certain areas.

"It makes sense to me now," Mada said, acknowledging the name of the county and also the school's mascot. There even were sections of land nearby which were preserved for them. Which come to think about it was probably ancient burial grounds from when they were slaughtered by the pilgrims, he thought.

The mention of the name reversal made him think about his father and how he had come to do the same thing with his name, having wanting to show his praises to the Lord in a town that frowned upon Christianity. The thought made him smile knowing now that his safety was his father's number one priority. As he was caught up in his own thoughts, he could hear Venus talking to Dolores and informing her of the chilling news which she had only come to know about not even a half hour ago. The sound of the coffee mug shattering as it landed onto the kitchen and the sight of the coffee spilling everywhere brought him back to reality. Dolores had taken the news in the same fashion as her daughter, which made him feel kind of guilty in a way being the bearer of bad news.

Immediately, Venus and he were by her side trying to consult and comfort her.

"Do you mean to tell me that this whole time I've been living among the very same people that hurt me?" Dolores questioned with disbelief and fear to her words. "I can't believe this. I just can't believe this. Who knows how many times I have crossed paths with these people and not have even known it." Her anger was now building inside of her.

"I'm sorry, Mama. I know that this is hard for you right now," Venus said in her most soothing voice possible. Her own eyes were beginning to tear up again at the sight of her mother breaking down from what she was just told.

Mada could only just stand there in silence, feeling the pain and hurt which the two women were feeling with, and trying to think of something to say as a solution to help ease the pain.

"I think that we should all get away for the day and do something fun and exciting to distract our minds from all of this bad news," he finally said as he finished cleaning up the spilled coffee and the shards of the broken mug. The words which were printed on it said, "#1 Mom, you are my world," and knowing that this was a gift from Venus tore him up inside. For it was through Dolores's hardship which she had endured that she was able to give Venus the gift of life. And he knew deep down inside that this was a choice that not many women would've made knowing the circumstances of it all.

"I left you wanting to see some animals last night, so how about I make up for it and we all hear it to the zoo today," Mada spoke to the ladies. "It'll be my treat as a token of appreciation to have you both in my life."

The comment made them both smile, and they agreed that some time away could do them all some good for the day. As they went to change and prepare themselves for their outing, Mada could only sit on the sofa in the living room and give thought to all that had been transpiring in his life, especially within the last couple of weeks.

"Welcome to the county zoo. Today is women Wednesday," the ticket receptionist said, informing them that every Wednesday for the month was half price for all the women to show thanks for all that they have overcome. The three of them all looked at one another with surprise in their eyes at hearing this.

"Did you know about that special?" Venus asked Mada curiously.

"No, not at all, Vee, but I guess that destiny is on our side as of lately. Now what do you ladies say that we get up in here and have ourselves the time of our lives?" he said, putting his arms out sideways in a V formation so that he could escort each one into the zoo as a trio.

"Ooh, Mama, look at the giraffes," Venus said in exclamation, sounding like a little child as they strolled through the zoo. Seeing how happy they were and seeing how much of a good time they were having together made him proud for deciding to have this outing with them. They were able to feed and hold some baby alligators, touch some snakes and snap nurse sharks, and even got to do some zip lining afterward as a bonus. All in all, they had the perfect day. With each one of the ladies being able to find a loose plume from one of the many peacocks that roamed around the grounds of the zoo freely among all of the pedestrians.

"Thank you for the day, Mada," Dolores said, wanting to give thanks and appreciation for helping her occupy her mind and giving her a distraction over everything. "You're something special."

"Yeah, Mada, you see, I told you that you were special," Venus agreed with her mother as she playfully tickled at his nose with her feather.

"I've been hearing that a lot as of lately," he said. "And don't worry, the pleasure was all mine, and I should be the one thanking you for making this more meaningful by gracing me with the company."

They loaded into the car and headed back home to face reality once again.

CHAPTER 11

As for you, you were dead in your transgressions and sins, in which you use to live when you followed the ways of the world and the ruler of the kingdom of the air, the Spirit who is now at work in those who are disobedient. All of us also loved among them at one time, gratifying the cravings of our flesh and following its desires and thoughts. Like the rest, we were by nature deserving of wrath. But because of his great love for us, God, who is rich in mercy, made us alive with Christ even when we were dead in transgressions—it is by Grace you have been saved. (Ephesians 2:1–5)

Jesus, full of the holy spirit, left to Jordan and was led by the spirit into the wilderness, where for forty days (sand amount of time as the great floods) he was tempted by the devil. He ate nothing during those days, and at the end of them he was hungry. The devil said to him, "If you are the son of God, tell this stone to become bread." Jesus answered, "It is written: 'Man shall not live on bread alone." The devil led him up to a high place and showed him in an instant all the kingdoms of the world. And days to him, "I will give you authority and splendor; it has been given to me, and I can give it to anyone I want to. If you worship me, it will all be yours. Jesus answered, "It is written: "Worship the Lord your

God and serve him only.' The devil led him to Jerusalem and had him stand on the highest point of the temple. "If you are the son of God," he said, "throw yourself down from here." For it is written: "He will command his angels concerning you to guard you carefully; They will lift you up in their hands, so that you will not strike your foot to the rest.' When the devil has finished all this tempting, he left until an opportune time. (Luke 4:1–13)

The battle of the gods would go on in this manner in the times of past for quite a while. From the uprisings and fake off kings to the creation of false idols of worship and even the existence of different religions. The Spirit of evil would not stop at nothing in order to turn the world against the Spirit of good.

And although there may have been times when it seemed as if evil was winning, good was always on the rise to place a foothold on all wickedness and sin that evil could come up with. For the power of good will always prevail.

CHAPTER 12

Then they said to Jeremiah, "May the Lord be a true and faithful witness against us if we do not act in accordance with everything the Lord your God sends you to tell us. Whether it is favorable or unfavorable, we will obey the Lord our God, to whom we are sending you, so that it will go well with us, for we will obey the Lord our God. (Jer. 42:5–6)

"Welcome back, brethren. It is good to be among you all as we gather here today in the house of worship praising the Almighty Father from the heavens above," said Reverend McNeilson as the people of the church entered and took their seats among the pews. For some reason, the crowd was in abundance today as the reverend continued.

"Today I tell you, my brothers and sisters, that the enemy is among us, and he is stronger than ever," the reverend continued. "I tell you that even at this very moment, he is here within the very church. If you don't believe me, just go into your pockets or purses and feel for your phones.

"From the days of before when he was granted authority of the airwaves, he had been busy visiting many homes and lives. From the invention of the radio to the TV, the computer, and now these smart phones, I tell you, my brothers and sisters, that Satan had been destroying lives, ruining marriages, and corrupting the world. And sad to say but also the truth, it is only going to get worse for us and easier for him as we continue in advancement with technology. What would take days, weeks, months, and sometimes longer is now reaching within minutes or second thanks to emails, faxes, and text.

"This is why, my brothers and sisters, I tell you that now more than ever, we must seek out God. Not only seek him but also speak of him—anywhere and everywhere whenever we can. We must deliver the Gospel just as fast and if not faster than technology."

The congregation broke out in cheers, praises to the Holy One, and encouraging Reverend McNeilson to continue with his powerful sermon.

"I'll go out on a limb and say that I'm sure most of us know what an acronym is, and for those who don't, well, you're going to learn today," he said.

"USA, PIN#, LOL, or TTYL, to name a few, which I'm sure you know already. Now here are two that we all should have known way before some of those," the reverend continued. "BIBLE, basic instructions before leaving earth. And JESUS, joined earth to save us with salvation."

At hearing these, the crowd in the congregation rose one by one until there was a standing ovation among the church. And with that, the choir joined the reverend on the altar and began with their own rendition of "Amazing Grace." As the church sang along with the choir, Mada had found himself in his own thoughts thinking of his father and how he had come up with an acronym for his name from what his mother had told him.

Majestic angel derived from Adam. Oh, good many times he had heard these words in his dreams even he would have his visions of his father Yosef, whose name in itself translated to I AM.

Yosef DeSol, I am of the sun, he thought as the song came to an end, along with the service for the day.

The line to the exit was extralong due to the overcrowding of the church today but also because there were so many people praising the reverend and thanking him as he shook their hands while they were leaving.

"What do you ladies say to a good brunch at the Pancake House?" Mada asked them as they stood in line nearing the exit slowly but surely.

"Right about now, that sounds delicious," Venus said.

"And not having to worry about cooking ourselves, or doing any dishes sounds great too," Dolores followed, giving her sign of approval to the idea. As they neared the reverend, Mada decided that he would also invite him to tag along to give him gratitude for such a great service. Also thinking that he would appreciate being among people outside of church considering that his wife had passed away two years previously due to a long battle with cancer.

"Oh, why, certainly I would love to join you all," the reverend said, remembering to himself how he and his wife would do the very same thing themselves when she was alive.

"And if it's okay with you two, and, Dolores, if you wouldn't mind either, you're more than welcome to ride along with me," he offered, not wanting to have to drive alone.

"No, we don't mind at all," Mada said, speaking for Venus as well as he gave her a sign that they would smoke on the way there now that Dolores wouldn't be in the car.

They took off right away down the back roads toward RT 60 before turning left and heading toward US 1 and nearing the Pancake House. They had arrived first due to the reverend having to close the church up and decided that they would enter and ask for a table for a while so that the wait to be served wouldn't be any longer than necessary. As they sat, they talked about the service and how deep the reverend had been getting into topics and also about how full the church was.

"That is something that drew me and caught my attention," Mada spoke. "Saying such a grand mixture of people, of all ages, ethnicities, race, color, and creed celebrating among one another so freely leaves me in awe. It makes me think about water."

Venus inquired what he had meant by that saying.

"Well, we have fresh water, saltwater, rainwater, and even brackish waters. But one thing about them all is that they all flow fluidly in the path of least resistance, and upon the moment which they meet, no matter how it may occur, they all mesh well. You do not see the ocean spitting the rains back out or the rivers shying away from the streams. So, therefore, if people were like the waters, I believe that there would automatically be more respect and peace in this world. Which ultimately would equal to a better and happier place to live in," he finished up.

All this mumbo jumbo left her with her jaw wide open seeing how it all made perfect sense.

"I tell you what, boy. Whoever said that weed dumbs you down needs to sit down with you sometime. Smoke a blunt with you and just begin talking to see what kind of conversation you'll have," Venus said, giving him kudos for how his mind worked. Right at that moment, the reverend and Dolores were making their way in through the front entrance, to which she raised her hand and waved in order to get their attention so that they would all be joined at the table. As they ate and talked among each other about anything and everything, they heard a horn honking from outside. Dolores, being the closest one to the window, had the best vote to see what all the commotion was about.

"That poor man is going to get himself killed if he's not more careful running back and forth in those streets collecting change," she said, knowing what he was doing, for she herself has given him a dollar while the reverend had waited on the red light to turn green so that they could enter the parking lot to the Pancake House.

"You should see his little gimmick which he uses to catch people's attention and also say thank you too," she continued to speak. "It's the cutest little horn that makes the pitiest of squeaks as if the bulb of it is broken." At hearing her words, Mada's fork, along with the piece of waffle the was on it, dropped and clashed onto his plate.

"What did you just say?" he asked her, not really needing for her to reiterate but just wanting confirmation. This bit of information was something that he had only told the detective the day which they met, and it was only because there had been nothing else of use that he could provide Detective Richards with.

"Will you all excuse me for a moment? I need to grab something from my car," he said, rising and moving rapidly toward the exit sign. His heart was now racing like pistons of a car that was doing well over a hundred miles per hour. His thoughts going just as fast as he rummaged through the center console seeking out the small business card. His hands shook as he looked out through his windshield at the man panhandling.

"Is it you?" Mada spoke to himself as he scanned the area and also looked the man over multiple times before beginning to punch in the numbers from the card into his cell phone. The resemblances were there, but he had wanted to be 100 percent correct before entering the last digit into his phone. As he watched the older gentlemen who in fact did have a salt-and-pepper beard and also the horn in his hand, he prayed to God.

"Please, Lord, give me a sign for confirmation before I bother the detective for nonsense," he spoke to the heavens. He exited his car in hopes of getting a little closer without being noticed when he got his sign from the Heavenly Father.

"Thanks, young blood," he had heard the panhandler say to the kid who had just given him some change in his cup. The gentleman squeezed his horn and the little boy's face, causing the kid to smile before he himself began to walk toward the sidewalk for the light was just about to change. As he did so, Mada got the rest of his confirmation when he had noticed the bicycle propped up against the street post, and this is when he entered the final number into his phone.

"This is Richards," the voice on the other end said after the second ring. Mada informed him of their location and of the gentleman as he kept his eyes on the individual, not wanting to lose him.

"All right, don't go and do anything foolish, Mr. DeSol. I can be there in less than ten minutes," detective Richards said before hanging up his phone without even saying a goodbye.

"Please hurry," Mada spoke to himself as he went back into his car to be discreet but also to be able to have a good view of the man until the detective would arrive. To him, the minutes felt like hours as he waited in his car not even wanting to blink from all the adrenaline rushing through his body at this very moment. He was so caught up in his own that he jumped in his seat, not noticing Venus as she opened the passenger side door.

"Boy, you couldn't wait until we finish eating to come smoke some more weed?" she asked, still not knowing what was now unfolding before their very eyes.

"Look over there across the street by the lamp post," he said as he pointed the man out to her.

"Is that him, Mada?" she asked, her words filled with terror and fright as she now sat staring at one of the men who had caused so much suffering on her mother and who could quite possibly be her very own father. Just then, Mada's phone began to ring, and he answered it upon the first ring, noticing that the number which he was looking at was that of the detective's.

"Hello? Yes, sir, we're outside in my car, and, yeah, he is still around," Mada answered the questions. While still on the phone, he had noticed the detective's car pulling into the lot.

"That's him right over there, sir. I'm 100 percent certain of it," he told Mr. Richards as he watched the bum preparing to make his next rounds from car to car in hopes of scoring some more money for who knows what.

"All right, you guys just sit tight right here while I go handle the situation," the detective said as he headed across the street in the direction of the man. Detective Richards escorted him off the street and back toward the sidewalk before finally retrieving his set of handcuffs and detaining the suspect. Upon seeing his arrest, Mada decided that there was nothing else which they could now do and suggested that they return inside to join Dolores and the reverend to finish their meals.

"I'm sure that he'll be in touch with us soon enough," he said as he held the door open for Venus.

"There you two are," Reverend McNeilson said as they joined them back at the table. "You guys are like magicians, always disappearing." He made a joke of how they were quick to vanish.

"Let's just say that we were doing the work of God while at the same time fulfilling justice," Mada said, receiving an "Amen to that" from them both, unbeknown to them of what had just took place outside while they ate their food inside.

"I'll take care of the bill, and if you wouldn't mind, Reverend, you can take care of the tip," he said as he got up and walked over to the lady by the register. They all said their formalities to one another before loading into his car and preparing to head back toward

Wabasso. It couldn't have been no more than ten minutes of driving when his phone went off again. He answered the immediately once seeing the now recognizable and memorized number. The detective had asked if they would be willing to stop by the precinct to identify the man as the suspect from the night at the store. Little did he know that they would also be coming with the victim of the cold case which he had now been working on.

"Dolores, there is something we need to tell you," Mada spoke after hanging up the phone, not wanting to spring any unnecessary and sudden surprises upon her and wanting to prepare her for what was about to come. With that, he said, "I'll leave the rest up to you, Vee," and continued to drive as he inputted the precinct's address into his phone's GPS.

"Mama, they just caught the man who raped you," she brought it out quickly without any soft preparation as to what her mother was about to hear. Dolores just sat there in silence with a stunned and shocked look across her face. The look showed that she was lost in her thoughts, and before you knew it, the teardrops began to stream down her golden face onto her lap.

"Would you like for me to take you home first, Dolores, before we go and meet up with detective to confirm the identity of the assailant?" he asked, wanting to give her the opportunity to decide whether or not she would want to come face-to-face with one of the men who had violated her almost three decades ago.

"No, I want to go with. I need to go with," she said, trying to sound as strong as possible. But one could still make out the hurt in her tone of voice.

The Indian River County Sheriff's Office was located in the town of Gifford, which had actually happened to be not so far from where their location was now. And therefore, for the remainder of their ride, they ended up driving in silence. Not due to the fact that they had nothing to talk about but because they all each happened to be in their own minds and thoughts preparing for what was about to take place upon making it to the sheriff's office.

"Thank you for coming so quickly on such short notice," Detective Richards said from the front door entrance to the building, for he had decided to wait for their arrival outside.

"Good afternoon, ladies," he said, acknowledging both Venus and Dolores coming along with him. Mada introduced them all but left out the part of whom they had happened to be. They entered into the brightly lit building and could feel a sudden chill as a temperature inside was easily ten degrees or more colder than the warmth which was felt outside from the Florida sun.

"Right this way," the detective spoke, leading them all into a room down the hallway and informing them that the glass was mirrored on the other side. So they had no need of worrying that they would be seen.

He then exited and shortly thereafter appeared on the other side of the glass as he entered that room with the man in tow. Mada watched the ladies as they just looked at this person through the glass, and he wondered what they both could be thinking of or feeling at this very moment. He then looked over to the gentleman himself and scanned him over as well. He could not see any real resemblance in the guy in comparison to Venus, but still he knew that this didn't exactly take him out of the equation as to possibly being her father. Mada then glanced down and saw something peculiar that stuck out to him like a sore thumb, no pun intended. But the man had Band-Aids on his left ankle and toes. Upon seeing this, he knew within himself that he was now staring at one of the men who had caused Dolores so much heartache and pain for all these years, transforming her life to one of a recluse, living like a hermit in fear of wanting to step out of her home, but only when really necessary and for church. Knowing this made him feel guilt for Dolores and anger toward this man who just a couple of weeks ago was a complete stranger whom he didn't even know existed in this world. As he looked the guy over once more, he was overcome with a sense of joy knowing that justice would finally be served after so many years. And he just hoped deep down within himself that Dolores may now finally be able to regain her life back.

"That's our man, ladies," Mada said, giving them full confirmation to the question that weighed on their minds. Not too long afterward did the detective reenter the room which where they were and looked over toward Mada.

No words were exchanged but only the slightest of head nod.

"All right, well, as of right now, this guy doesn't even know what's in store for him. He just thinks that some good Samaritan gave a complaint on him for panhandling in the streets," the detective said to them all.

"What's his name?" Dolores asked, being the first one to speak out of the three.

"Payne, Max Major Payne," replied Mr. Richards. The irony of his words settling into Mada's mind as he thought of the commonality of this guy's name in comparison to Dolores's name, which led him to believe that Venus was in fact a true miracle baby. Or better yet, a child of God.

"So who gets to break the bad news to him?" Venus asked, wanting to be able to tell this man that he would never get to see the light of day on the streets again.

"Sorry, Ms. De La Crux, as much as I would love to grant you the privilege to be the bearer of bad news, that is something which is left to us here in the department. But you will get your chance to speak your mind to him when he goes to court," Detective Richard said, now being aware that Dolores was the victim to the heinous crime of yesteryears. "There's one more thing that I want to ask of you, though, Venus, before you guys may be on your way. Would you mind giving us a blood sample so that we may see if this guy could possibly be your father?"

The question being one that he didn't want to ask but had to ask due to protocol.

"Yes," she answered, wanting to know for herself if she was in fact looking at her father for the first and quite possibly what could be the last time in her life.

The tube of blood was drawn, and then they were off headed back toward home solemnly, but at the same time with a sense of peace.

CHAPTER 13

How deserted lies the city, once so full of people! How like a widow is she, who once was great among the nations! She who was Queen among the provinces has now become a slave. literally she weeps at night, tears are on her cheeks. Among all her lovers there is no one to come for her. All her friends have betrayed her; they have become her enemies. after affliction and harsh labor, Judah has gone into exile. She dwells among the nations; she finds no resting place. All who pursue her have overtaken her in the midst of her distress. The roads to Zion mourn, for no one comes to her appointed festivals. Or her gateways are desolate, her priest groan, her young woman grieve, and she is in bitter anguish. Her foes have become her masters; her enemies are at ease. The Lord has brought her grief because of her many sins. Her children have gone into exile, captive before the foe. All the splendor has departed from daughter Zion. Her princess are like deer that find no pasture; in weakness they have fled before the pursuer. In the days of her affliction and wandering Jerusalem remembers all the treasures that were hers in the days of old. When her people fell into enemy hands, there was no one to help her. Her enemies looked at her and laughed at her destruction. Jerusalem has seen greatly and so has become unclean.

Or who honored her despise her, for they have all seen her naked; she herself groans and turns away. Her filthiness clung to her skirts; she did not consider her future. Her fall was astounding; there was none to comfort her. "Look, Lord, on my affliction, for the enemy has triumphed." The enemy laid hands on all her treasures; she saw pagan nations enter her sanctuary-those you had forbidden to enter your assembly. All her people groan as they search for bread; they barter their treasures for food to keep themselves alive. Look, Lord, and consider, for I am despised." "Is it nothing to you, all you who pass by? Look around and see. Is any suffering like my suffering that was inflicted on me, that the Lord brought on me in the day of his fierce anger? "From on high he sent fire, sent it down into my bones. He spread a net for my feet and turned me back. He made me desolate, faint all the day long. "My sins have been bound into a yoke; by his hands they were woven together. They have been hung on my neck, and the Lord has sapped my strength. He has given me into the hands of those I cannot withstand. "The Lord has rejected all the warriors in my midst; he has summoned an army against me to crush my young men. And his wine press the Lord has trampled virgin daughter Judah. "This is why I weep and my eyes overflow with tears. No one is near to comfort me, no one to restore my spirit. My children are destitute because the enemy has prevailed." Zion stretches out her hands, but there is no one to comfort her. The Lord has decreed for Jacob that his neighbors become his foes; Jerusalem has become an unclean thing among them. "The Lord is righteous, yet I rebelled against his command. Listen, all you peoples; lol on my suffering. My young man and young woman have gone into exile. "I called to my allies but they betrayed me. My priest and my elders perished in the city while they searched for food to keep themselves alive. "See, Lord how the stress I am! I am in torment within, and in my heart I am disturbed, for I have been most rebellious. Outside, the sword bereaves; Inside, there is only death. "People have heard my groaning, but there is no one to comfort me. All my enemies have heard of my distress; they rejoice at what you have done. May you bring the day you have announced so they may become like me. "Let all their wickedness come before you; deal with dumb as you have dealt with me because of all my sins. My groans are many and my heart is faint." (Lam. 1:1–22)

These were the cries and pleas of the spirit of evil as she suffered and realized that the spirit of goodness was too strong and powerful to compete against. Knowing of the Lord's love and everlasting kindness, she prayed out to him in vain seeking to be shown mercy. Praying for mercy now as she once did in the very beginning of life when she was once a true believer. The only difference now being that these were crocodile tears as she patiently waited for her spirit to strengthen again as people believed in her once more.

CHAPTER 14

Then they asked him, "What must we do to do the works God requires?" Jesus answered, "The work of God is this: to believe in the one he has sent." So they asked him, "What sign then will you give that we may see it and believe you? What will you do? Our ancestors ate the manna in the wilderness; as it is written: 'He gave them bread from heaven to eat.' Jesus said to them, "Very truly I tell you, it is not Moses who had given you the bread from heaven, but it is my Father who gives you the true bread from heaven. "For the bread of God is the bread that comes down from heaven and give life to the world." "Sir," they said, "always give us this bread." Then Jesus declared, "I am the bread of life. Whoever comes to me whenever go hungry, and whoever believes in me Will never be thirsty. But as a told you, you have seen me in still you do not believe. All those the father gives me will come to me, and whoever comes to me I will never drive away. For I have come down from heaven not to do my will but to do the will of him who sent me. And this is this the will of him who sent me, that I shall lose none of all those he has given me, but raise them up at the last day. For my father's will is that everyone who looks to the Son and believes in him shall have eternal life, and I will raise them up at the last day." (John 6:28–40)

Mada woke up feeling positive about the day. He was in such good spirit having being able to get in a full night's worth of uninterrupted sleep again. He was beginning to have more of these nights more often. And therefore he decided that he would get to the gym early again, for it had actually been a while since he was able to go having so much on his mind and dealing with everything that he was going through.

"This is definitely my second favorite hobby," he talked to himself as he viewed himself in the wall-size mirror of the gym. Today he found himself doing a combination of pull-ups, pushups, and dips. Although strenuous, he enjoyed this routine quite a bit for it focused on numerous body parts all at the same time. And today he could really see that his hard work and dedication have been paying off well. His body was chiseled like one of those stone statues of gods, emperors, and legendary figures which you see in museums, cathedrals, and movies. But for him, what he enjoyed the most from his workouts was that feeling of satisfaction when he'd walked out of the gym after being done. This feeling would dissipate his stresses and leave him feeling great and more positive and optimistic way. The only other thing in this world that could put him in this state of mind was the Christian music which he listened to so often, minus the strenuous part, of course.

Although, having to battle evil within the mind could be one heck of a battle within itself that could leave a person feeling zapped and the body drained of energy of the desire to do anything. He was digging for his car keys in his pocket when his phone began to ring in the other one. He quickly grabbed his keys and then swapped over his gym bag so that he may retrieve his phone with the other hand now. He answered it on the fourth ring without taking any notice to whom was calling him.

"Hello," he said, speaking into the phone as he fumbled with the keys, gym bag, and car door all at once trying to get situated into his car.

"Good morning, Mr. DeSol, how are you doing, and do you have a few minutes to spare?" Detective Richards spoke from the other end. No introduction really needed, for Mada could tell whom it was because nobody else who called him would use his last name when reaching out to him.

"Yeah, sure, just give me a second," he replied as he threw the gym bag into the passenger seat and inserted the key fob into the ignition.

"What is it, sir?" he asked, having been a few days since they last spoke after the arrest of Mr. Payne.

"Well, I have some good news, some sad news, and also some disturbing news for you. Now I just need to know which one you would like to hear first, Mr. DeSol?" the detective asked.

Mada, still feeling upbeat from his workout, decided that he'd like to hear it in reverse order from the way which it was offered to him. He figured that if he was going to be given an option, that he would have whatever was to come out of this conversation finish in a positive note.

"Very well then, sir," the detective began. "Today and early hours of the morning, Mr. Payne was pronounce dead. He was found by a correctional officer hanging from a light fixture in his cell."

"Oh my god," Mada said upon hearing this.

"Shall I continue, Mr. DeSol?" the detective asked, not sure if Mada wanted to hear any more of what was to be told. Figuring to himself that this must have been the worst of it all, he told the detective to carry on.

"The sad news being that today we also received the results from forensic regarding the testing done from the blood taken from Ms. De La Crux, and it was a positive match, sir."

Once again, "Oh my god" were the only words that Mada could speak before Detective Richards moved on to the last bit of information.

"Please, Lord, let this really be some good news," he prayed to himself as the detective spoke.

"So although that Mr. Payne was being uncooperative upon his initial arrest, he was considerate enough to leave a suicide note. It turns out that the other individual who abetted in the crime had happened to die from a drug overdose. And get this," he continued, "he died on the same night of the assault. We were able to verify this through the obituary logs, and the irony of it all is that they used the money which they stole from Ms. De La Crux to purchase the drugs."

"Oh my god, talk about instant karma," Mada said upon hearing the rest of what the detective needed to say. Instantly, his mind began to race on how he would break all this new information to both Venus and Dolores. The latter of it all making him feel good knowing that Dolores could now very well pick up the pieces of the puzzle and put her life back together again.

"You sound like a very religious man from your responses, Mr. DeSol. I am too, and I'll go out on a limb and say that God took care of this one," the detective spoke.

Upon hearing that the detective was also a man of faith, Mada decided to extend an invitation to him to attend service with them sometime and gave him the name and location of the church.

"Bring your family along too. I think that they'll like it."

Mada decided that he would keep the information told to him from Detective Richards to himself for a few days. He did not want to keep burdening the ladies with bad news and had wanted to allow them some time to recover from everything else that they were still dealing with. In order to not feel guilty with himself about it, he decided that he would take a trip by himself down south to Miami. After all, he had been meaning to see what things were like down there since he first relocated to Florida from New York. He reached out to Venus at her job to let her know that he would be gone until Saturday evening but that he would be there to pick them up for service on Sunday. With that, he went home, packed a couple of outfits into his gym bag, grabbed his wooden box of smoking goodies, and found himself on 95 south for two and a half hours on a wild and sporadic road trip. He booked himself a nice hotel along the shoreline of South Beach upon reaching his destination. Right away, he noticed the difference in atmosphere and environment in comparison to what life was like living in Vero Beach. Miami was definitely more upbeat and fast-paced with a younger crowd as well. It kind of reminded him of New York, without the rats or as much trash either, though. Not sure what this trip would resolve or accomplish, he told himself that he would make the best of it either way.

CHAPTER 15

He said to me, "Son of man, stand up on your feet and I will speak to you." As he spoke, the Spirit came into me and raised me to my feet, and I heard him speaking to me. He said: "Soon of man, hi am sending you two the Israelites, to a rebellious nation that has rebelled against me; they and their ancestors have been in revolt against me to this very day. The people to who I am sending you are obstinate and stubborn. Say to them, 'This is what the Sovereign Lord says.' And whether they listen or fail to listen— for they are rebellious people—they will know that a prophet has been among them. And you, son of man, do not be afraid of what they say or be terrified by them, though they are a rebellious people. You must soak my words to them, weather day listen or fail to listen, for their rebellious. "But you, son of man, listen to what I say to you. Do not rebel like the rebellious people; open your mouth and eat what I give you." Then I looked, and I saw a hand stretched out to me. In it was a scroll, which he unrolled before me. On both sides of it were written words of lament and mourning and woe. And he said to me, "Son of man, eat this scroll I am giving you and fill your stomach with it." So I ate, and it tasted as sweet as honey in my mouth. (Ezek. 2:1–10, 3:1)

"Hey, Vee, how's it going?" Mada asked as he drove up North 95 headed back toward home. "I was wondering if you would like to join me for a smoke session down by the river?"

She accepted his offer and waited patiently for him to arrive.

"You know what, Mada, it must be nice to have enough money to not have to work and to be able to do as you please whenever you'd like," Venus said as he pulled into one of the few vacant spots down by the river.

"It helps, Vee, but to be honest, I'd rather live how God has intended for us to live," he said. "You see, money was one of mankind's many inventions. It was designed to make people think that it was a necessity in life in order to live. Sadly enough, many people in this day and age feel that it is a must-have, and of course, the more you have, the better off in life one is. And this might seem true, but only because people allow for themselves to feel this way. Listen, Vee, God intended for us to be farmers and live off the land."

This comment made her laugh.

"I'm serious, and I can explain why," Mada said, preparing to get more in-depth with what he was telling her. "From the beginning, if you read the Bible, God put Adam and Eve out into the lands after he cast them out of the garden of Eden. From that day forward, they were to work the grounds planting, fertilizing, and maintaining their field in order to produce crops and a harvest to live off. The only thing is that people became lazy and chose not to work the lands. You see, we were all supposed to be entitled to a section of land to cultivate and provide for our families in order to survive. The sluggard decided to allow their lands to go to waste or to sell it off to those who work and became their slaves for a meal."

Venus listened in amazement as he put these words together, nodding her head up and down in agreeance as it was making perfect sense to her.

"Please continue," she said.

"In this world, there is truly only four things which mankind really needs in order to live, and I will tell you them in order of what's needed the most. First and foremost is air, for without it, a person dies within minutes. Which is why in the Bible it speaks so often about the breath of man. Secondly, and this is also something which is mentioned many times in the good book, is water. And this is why astronomers also seek it out on other planets. Without water, mankind dies of thirst within a week or so. Third, Vee, is food. We need to eat so that we feed our bodies with energy. Without food, a person starves to death in about a month. And lastly, what mankind needs is clothing to protect us from the elements. Whether hot or cold. Everything else extra is invented by man, including that money, Vee. And if you really think about it, it's a way of making us modern-day slaves, because we work to give it away, paying for what God had intended to be free. We have water bills, grocery bills, and utility bills. Do you see the big picture now?" Mada asked her after what he felt was a lecture. "What I'd rather have more of and also what this world needs more of is *love*. Love would allow for us all to help one another out in times of need without expecting some type of payment. For a real favor is done for free, from the heart and not for funds. I could keep going for hours if not for days if you allow me to, Vee. But honestly, there is something else that I need to talk to you about, and the real reason that I had asked for you to come out here and smoke with me."

He then proceeded to tell her about Mr. Payne and all what Detective Richards had told him. On her face was a look of disbelief, hurt, and also pain. He could only imagine what was going on in her mind now.

"When did you find out about all of this?" she asked.

He was truthful and told her that he found out about it on the day that he decided to take his trip down to Miami, apologizing about it to her for having kept it a secret.

"I need to get home now. I need to talk to my mother," she said, asking for him to take her home and immediately. He didn't question her decision for he understood well where she was coming from.

"See you in the morning for church?" he asked her as she got out of the car.

She just gave him a nod and hurried into her house. With that, he drove home to unwind, unpack, and call it a night for it was a long day with the driving and all that just played out. That night, he dreamt of his father again.

"Solve the mystery about the girl," it started out as it normally did.

"How, Papa, how?" It continued as usual. The pattern was going on like it had so many times before.

"You have help now," his father said for the second time now since he had first begun having this dream as a child. But only this time, it went a little further than before.

"The end is near, my majestic angel. Don't let it be too late," his father said before a demonic figure came out from the shadows and snatched his father back into the dark abyss.

"Papa, nooo." Mada woke up screaming over and over covered in cold sweats. He was now full of even more confusion because he had thought that this dream had to do with Dolores and Venus.

"What do you mean that the end is near, and why did that evil creature take you away?" he asked himself, hoping that his father could somehow answer him now while he was awake.

At 5:00 a.m., he saw the time being as he looked at his phone. Also, there was a text from Venus, letting him know that he didn't need to pick them up for service after all, for they had decided that they would take the day to themselves but that he was more than welcome to come over after church if he had liked. He decided to make himself a good breakfast and take advantage of the extra hours by doing some laundry and cleaning up.

As he was pulling into the church parking lot, he was greeted by now too familiar face as well as a few new ones.

"Hello, Mr. DeSol. I decided to take you up on that offer from the other day. Please let me introduce you to my wife, Melissa Semone, and also our twin daughters, Destiny and Karma," Detective Richards said as Mada went near them.

"It's a pleasure to meet you all, and thank you for coming. I'm sure that you will enjoy the service. Reverend McNeilson is pretty amazing at what he does," Mada said. To which he then led them inside to be seated.

"Before we get started, I would like to welcome you all for coming out today and give you thanks on behalf of our Heavenly Father who watches in amazement from up above," the reverend said, commencing with the service. "I want to tell you all that we are dealing with a great epidemic, my brothers and sisters. An epidemic that exceeds HIV. An epidemic that is far more worse than cancer. If you listen to these words, I tell you that this epidemic is worse than COVID, polio, and the Black Plague combined, my brothers and sisters. And it has been going on since the very beginning of time. This epidemic which I speak of is called sin, and it is ending lives at a faster rate and scale than ever before. With that, I ask you all to turn to the fifth chapter of Genesis in your Bibles so that I may show you what I mean," the reverend continued.

"As you read this verses, I want you all to take a very good look at the numbers which represent the ages of how long mankind lived back then and then compare those numbers to the average lifespan of humans today. I'll give you all a minute or two to allow this figures to sink in, my brothers and sisters," he said.

"Not let us continue," he started again. "I tell you that the epidemic of sin has robbed mankind of living a life of longevity. If you don't believe me, just look into the next page chapter 6 verse 3, and you will read the Lord's spirit was so angry with mankind that he shortened our numbers of days down to a hundred and twenty years." "Compare that to Methuselah who lived for 969 years, or the first son Adam, who was also our first prophet, and he lived for a good 930 years. This is why, my brothers and sisters, I tell you that it isn't cancer, AIDS, or any plague that is killing us quicker. But our very own actions of wickedness and sin that has brought our days down so much." Reverend McNeilson continued as the house of God was now in an uproar of praises for the message which they were receiving.

"So I tell you here and now, brethren, it is sin and not any epidemic which has numbered our days. And to take from last week's service when I spoke of the airwaves, I will include that here now my great people. The advancement of technology, as good as it may seem when the newest gadget is invented, will be our very own demise to a shortened lifespan. And I tell you all here now, that if we allow this to continue and permit for sin to be right there in front of us, to continue to flourish at the touch of a button, I won't be surprised if mankind doesn't live a lifespan that passes fifty years of age in the near future," he said.

The congregation was once again in an uproar and giving him his second standing ovation in back-to-back weeks for such great and inspiring messages. All this made Mada thankful to have been introduced to the New Voice of God Church by Venus. And at the thought of her, he wished that they would have been here to take in this great service.

"Go ahead with your question, sister," the reverend said to the elderly lady in the front row of pews.

"How many years total did Eve live, Reverend?" she asked.

Mada had become lightheaded and dizzy as she asked the question, causing for him to have to take a quick seat so that he wouldn't topple over.

"Are you all right, Mr. DeSol?" Detective Richards asked him, seeing how he had gotten the same way which he had done the day that they first met by the store.

"Yeah, I'm okay. Just need to get myself a drink of water," Mada replied as he excused himself to head out toward the water fountain. He made sure to drink enough thinking that he was dehydrated from all the smoking that he does. As he was returning to the pews, he could hear the choir singing "Power in the Blood," which let him know that the service was nearing an end. As he opened the door to enter the congregational hall, he ran into the reverend who was preparing to greet everyone as they would begin to exit.

"Hello, Mada, how are you? God bless you, son," the reverend said, shaking his hand and then inquiring about Dolores and Venus.

Mada took it upon himself to tell the reverend why they were absent from service. After all, he was well aware of her ordeal being the one who had saved her life.

"Hey, Reverend, I had happened to step out to grab myself a bit of water and didn't get to hear you answer the sister's question in regard to Eve's age at her passing and would like to know," he asked.

"Well, my son of God, I wish that I could tell you, but truth be told, I don't have the answer. For it was never mentioned in the Bible," the reverend replied to his inquiry.

As Mada heard the reverend's response, his own father's word entered into his mind, *Solve the mystery about the girl, Mada,* and then he fainted and passed out.

CHAPTER 16

How the Lord has covered daughter Zion with the cloud of his anger! He has hurled down the splendor of Israel from Heaven to Earth; he has not remembered his footstool in the day of his anger. Without pity the Lord has swallowed up all the dwellings of Jacob; in his wrath he has torn down the strongholds of daughter Judah. He has brought her kingdom and it's princes down to the ground and dishonor. In fierce anger he has cut off every horn of Israel. He has withdrawn his right hand at the approach of the enemy. He has burned in Jacob like a flaming fire that consumes everything around it. Like an enemy he has strung his bow; his right hand is ready. Like a foe he has slain all who were pleasing to the eye; he has poured out his wrath like fire on the 10th of daughter Zion. The Lord is like an enemy; he has swallowed up all her palaces and destroyed her strongholds. He has multiplied morning and lamentation for daughter Judah he has laid waste his dwelling like a garden; he has destroyed his place of meeting.

The Lord has made Zion forget her appointed festivals and her sabbaths; in his fierce anger he has spurned both King and priests. The Lord has rejected his altar and abandoned his sanctuary. He has given the walls of her palaces into the hands of the enemy; they have raised a shout in the house of the Lord as on the day of an appointed festival. The Lord determined to tear down the wall around Daughter Zion. He stretched out a measuring line and did not withhold his hand from destroying. He made ramparts and walls lament; together they wasted away. Her Gates have sunk into the ground; their bars he has broken and destroyed. Her King and her princes are exiled among the nations, the law is no more, and her prophets no longer find visions from the Lord. The elders of daughter Zion sit on the ground and silence; they have sprinkled dust on their heads and put on sackcloths. The young woman of Jerusalem have bowed their heads to the ground. My eyes fail from weeping, I am in torment within; my heart is poured out on the ground because my people are destroyed, because children and infants faint in the streets of the city. They say to their mothers, "where is bread and wine?"

As they faint like the wounded in the streets of the city, as their lives ebb away in their mother's arms. What can I say for you? With what can I compare you, Daughter Jerusalem? To what can I liken you, that I may comfort you, Virgin Daughter Zion? Your wound is as deep as the sea. Who can heal you? Divisions of your prophets were false and worthless; they did not expose your sin to ward off your captivity. The prophecies they gave you were false and misleading. All who pass your way clap their hands at you; they scoff and shake their heads at daughter Jerusalem: "is this the city that was called the perfection of beauty, the joy of the whole earth?" All your enemies open their mouths wide against you: they scoff and gnash their teeth and say, "we have swallowed her up. This is the day we have waited for; we have lived to see it." The Lord has done what he planned; he has fulfilled his word, which he declared long ago. He has overthrown you without pity, he has let the enemy gloat over you, he has exalted the horn of your foes. The heart of the people cry out to the lord. Your walls of daughter Zion, let your tears flow like a river day and night; give yourself no relief, your eyes no rest. Arise, cry out in the night, as the watches of the night begin; pour out your heart like water in the presence of the lord.

Lift up your hands to him for the lives of your children, who faint from hunger at every street corner. "Look," Lord, and consider: whom have you ever treated like this? Should woman eat their offspring, the children they have cared for? Should priests and prophet be killed in the sanctuary of the lord? "Young and old lie together in the dust of the streets; My young men and young women have fallen by the sword. You have slain them in the day of your anger; you have slaughtered them without pity. "As you summon to a feast day, so you summoned against me terrors on every side. In the day of the Lord's anger no one escaped or survived; those I cared for and reared my enemy has destroyed. (Lam. 2:1–22)

These were yet more cries which the spirit of evil petitioned out to the Heavenly Father as she sought out mercy for the people who had worshiped her in the days of better times before the Mighty Lord and Savior of the earth released with wrath among the lands to cleanse the world once more of wickedness, evil, and sin. This has been the ways of the battles ever since the first time from when she first rebelled against our Great Father so long ago in the very garden of Eden. It is also the same way in which it is occurring in our present days as we speak. The spirits of good and evil battling one another among the world—the Lord from the heavens above and Satan from hell here on earth.

CHAPTER 17

His father Zechariah was filled with the holy Spirit and prophesied: "Praise be to the lord, the God of Israel, because he has come to his people and redeemed them. He has raised up a horn of salvation for us in the house of his servant David (as he said through his holy prophets of long ago), salvation from our enemies and from the hand of all who hate us—to show Mercy to our ancestors and to remember his holy covenant, the oath he swore to our Father Abraham: to rescue us from the hands of our enemies, and to enable us to serve him without fear in holiness and righteousness before him all our days. And you, my child, will be called a prophet of the most high; for you will go on before the Lord to prepare the way for him, to give his people the knowledge of salvation through the forgiveness of their sins, because of the tender mercy of our lord, by which the rising sun will come to us from heaven to shine on those living in darkness and in the shadow of death, to guide our feet into the path of peace."
(Luke 1:67–79)

"Hello, sleepyhead, I'm glad to see those beautiful eyes of yours open already," Venus said to Mada as she placed a kiss onto his forehead.

"What happened, and where am I?" he asked in confusion as he looked around trying to make sense of where he was at. As he glanced around the room little by little, he was beginning to understand that he happened to be somewhere that medical attention was performed. He was also able to put together a few other familiar faces among the strange ones like the nurses and orderlies whom were all dressed in white, leaving him thinking at first that he was in heaven and that they were angels preparing him to meet the Maker.

"Glad to have you back with us, my son," Reverend McNeilson said to him as he walked up behind Venus to also say hello to him. Following in tow behind the reverend was Dolores. She was holding some "Get well soon" balloons in one hand and the picture frame of the "old Indian," which he had commented on the first time he had entered into her home.

"I brought these for you hoping that they would bring you some comfort," she said as she placed them on his bedside table and then gave him a big loving hug in the way which a mother would hug a child in admiration. Seeing the three of them there gathered together in the room with him brought upon him a warm sensation of pride and love. For not too long ago, they were all strangers, yet here they were now giving him a feeling of once again having a family. This let him know that he truly wasn't alone anymore. And as he looked at the three of them, his own father's voice came into his mind as he heard, "You are not alone anymore. You have help," to which he faintly smiled.

"What time is it, and how long have you ask been here!" he asked, wanting to get a sense of how long he happened to be passed out. Vaguely remembering seeing the reverend's face last before he had entered what could only be considered and called a wild psyche-delic dream. Full of visions and images unlike any of the ones which he had had previously in the past.

"It's soon going to be four o'clock in the afternoon. And we came as soon as we could once the reverend had called and told us what had happened to you," Venus said as she grabbed a hold of his hand and gave it a big squeeze.

"Detective Richards had stopped by as well, wanting to see how you were holding up and to also thank you personally for having invited him to the church. He was on call duty, though, and therefore, he couldn't stay too long before having to leave, but he wanted to know that you have a new church brother among the congregation—that's how much he enjoyed the service today," the reverend said.

Right as he was done talking, one of the male orderlies came in and headed to his bed as well.

"So here is an update on all that we have done," he spoke. "There were no abnormalities in your brain function from the CAT scan which was performed. All the lab work from the blood testing had come back showing no negative results, and your heart rate and pulse both seem to be normal as well, Mr. DeSol. To be perfectly honest with you, we couldn't come up with the slightest of explanations as to why you passed out the way which you did for such a long period of time. And the only thing that we could come up with is stress," the orderly said, finishing up and trying to rationalize as to why Mada had went into a temporary coma-like stage.

"Maybe you should wean down on your marijuana intake as well," he added before heading back out of the room trying to suggest that this could have happened from his smoking.

"As if. I'm ready to get out of here now just so that I can finish the half a blunt which I left in my car from this morning before church," Mada said while then apologizing to the reverend from his confession.

"It's okay, son. To be perfectly honest with you, I think that even Jesus and his disciples partook of the wacky tobacky in the days of yonder. Shoot, I know that I did," the reverend said, causing for everyone to break out in a fit of laughter. Not too long after and Mada was signing his medical release papers so that he could be on his way. They also had him a prescription for a drug that would supposedly help out with his stress and another for vertigo. Both of which would end up torn into pieces and discarded into the trash receptacle that was right outside of the hospital entrance.

Mada was always opposed to the pharmaceutical companies and all their legal drugs. Drugs that by any other name would get a person incarcerated for who knew how long and all because big brother and Uncle Sam didn't have their hands in the cookie jar to tax it. Drugs like marijuana that was now being credited for all its natural remedies and has become so accepted throughout the nation and also the world. And only because the government seeing how lucrative it was. But also recalling the movies of the past like *Reefer Madness*, which made marijuana look worse than the devil himself.

Mushrooms now becoming the second runner-up for natural plants and substances, which is still in its developmental stages by big pharma companies that is now being praised for its hallucinogenic properties in micro dosages. If you ask me, the Indians knew what they were doing and talking about many years ago when they would do their rituals and spiritual dances speaking to the gods while under the influences Mada thought to himself as he followed behind the reverend and Dolores to his car.

Venus was right beside him, holding hands like two teenagers who were first beginning to experience puppy love.

"The food which we had prepared from earlier is probably cold by now, but it will only take but a few minutes to warm up in the microwave if you'd like to stay and eat, Reverend," Dolores said, extending an invitation for him to join them all for a lunch which had now become dinner. Having had skipped out on the service, they had taken the timeout to make some Spanish rice and beans with fried pork chops, empanadas, and also some fried sweet plantains. He took her up on the offer, and they all entered into the cozy little house which felt like a home. Mada chose to give thanks and praises for the meal which was now placed out in front of them all as they sat together around the table.

"First and foremost, I want to thank you, Lord, for these wonderful and amazing people which you have brought into my life and into my heart. It is due to them all in their own unique ways that I now feel blessed to have a family again, even if not by blood but through your spirit, Father God. Secondly, I want to thank you for my life and for having mercy upon me. For we all have seen in the past recent days how one can be here today and gone tomorrow. And last but not least, we all give thanks for this wonderful and delicious-smelling food which we are about to eat. May it suit us well, Lord. I could keep going, but I'm hungry as heck. Thank you, Amen," he said as they all laughed together again from his whimsical joke. They all enjoyed the foods as they talked, laughed, joked around, and listened to some music as one little happy team of friends and family.

"Can you give me a ride to my car?" Mada asked the reverend after they all enjoyed their dinner and the time spent together.

"Of course I can, son," he replied, finishing up with the dishes and gathering his things before they both would part ways from the ladies and head toward the church.

"Reverend, can I talk to you about anything without being judged by you?" Mada asked him as they drove in the car.

"Why, of course, my son, you may, and worry naught—for judgment can only come from the man up above."

Mada told him about the reoccurring dream with his father and also about his visions. He also told him about the dizzy spells which he gets every so often while being awake as it had happened today and how he thinks that there's a connection between everything.

"I have to agree with you, Mada, for you know that I told you that you were special from the first day that we met. I could just feel it as we shook hands, and although I couldn't figure it out then, I think that I know now, Mada," the reverend spoke to him.

"You are a seer, a true living prophet placed on this earth to do the works of God, my son, or shall I say, his son. I didn't see it before, but even your name saves it, Mada—just read it backward and you'll understand. The same way I take it that your father understood and knew. Which leads me to believe that this is why his life was taken." The reverend saying this made the hairs on both of their arms rise out of fear. As if they had just gotten the chills or something.

"I also tell you, Mada, that you didn't choose Florida but that the Almighty Creator chose Florida for you. He has been guiding you toward the path which he feels must be taken, the same way in which he had done so for Moses, for Abraham, and for so many other prophets which he had used their bodies in order to get his word out to the world. So that people may believe as they are told the message from the Heavenly Father," Reverend McNeilson said.

Mada couldn't believe all that he was hearing, but as he allowed for the reverend's words to play over and over in his mind, he could start making sense of it all.

"But I tell you this as well, Mada. The spirit of God is not the only spirit that enters people. The enemy is a copycat, and he mimics all that the Creator does. Wanting to be just like our Lord and Savior, but only for the sake of evil. There are even people just like you, Mada, seers, who have the same gift which you possess, but only they use it for the sake of wickedness and corruption. And sadly enough, they can even portray to be good when they are really not. Because after all, the spirit of evil used to once be an angel," Reverend McNeilson finished saying as he pulled into the parking lot beside Mada's car. At the sound of the reverend's last statement, Mada was left wondering if he himself had ever crossed paths with one of those types of people.

"Thank you for the ride, Reverend, and also for the words of wisdom which you have just shared with me."

"It was my pleasure, Mada. Now let me ask you something—would you be willing to go up on the podium with me next Sunday to help do the service?" he asked, catching Mada off guard with the question. "We'll keep your gift a secret from everyone, of course, but I think that it'll be truly amazing to have a real man of God speak to the congregation."

"You sure about this, Reverend? I've never stood in front of a crowd to speak before, let alone know where to begin," Mada said.

"Yes, I'm sure, Mada, and don't you worry, for even though it'll be you up in front of the crowd, it'll actually be the Heavenly Father providing you with the words which you'll need to say."

Mada thought for a second and then decided that he could not turn his back on God, no matter his fears.

"Sure, okay, Reverend, I'll do it," he said before wishing Bishop McNeilson a good night and headed home.

C H A P T E R   1 8

I am the man who has seen affliction by the rod of the Lord's wrath. He has driven me away and made me walk in darkness rather than light; Indeed, he has turned his hand against me again and again all day long. He has made my skin and my flesh grow old and has broken my bones. He has besieged me and surrounded me with bitterness and hardship. He has made me dwell in darkness like those long dead. He has walled me in so I cannot escape; he has weighed me down with chains. Even when I call out or cry for help, he shuts out my prayer. He has barred my way with blocks of stone; he has made my paths crooked. Like a bear lying in wait, like a lion in hiding, he dragged me from the path and mangled me and left me without help. He drew his bow and made me to target of his arrows. He pierced my heart with arrows from his quiver. I became the laughing stock of all my people; they mock me in song all day long. He has filled me with bitter herbs and given me gall to drink. He has broken my teeth with gravel; he has trampled me in the dust. I have been deprived of peace; I have forgotten what prosperity is. So I say, "My splendor is gone and all that I had hoped from the Lord." I remember my affliction and my wandering, the bitterness and the gall. I will remember them, and my soul is downcast within me. Yet this I call to mine and therefore I have hope. Because of the Lord's great love we are not consumed, for his compassions never fail. They are new every morning; great is your faithfulness. I say to myself, "The Lord is my portion; therefore I will wait for him." The Lord is good to those whose hope is in him, to the one who seeks him; it is good to wait quietly for the salvation of the lord. It is good for a man to bear the yoke while he is young. Let him sit alone in silence, for the Lord has laid it on him. Let him bury his face in the dust—there may yet be hope. Let him offer his cheek to one who would strike him, and let him be filled with disgrace. For no one is cast off by the Lord forever. Though he brings grief, he will show compassion, so great is his unfailing love. For he does not willingly bring affliction or grief to anyone. To crush on the foot all prisoners in the land, to deny people their rights before the Most High, to deprive them of Justice—would not the Lord see such things? Who can speak and have it happen if the Lord has not decreed it? Is it not from the mouth of the Most High that both calamities and good things come? Why should the living complain when punished for their sins? Let us examine our ways and test them, and let us return to the lord. Let us lift up our hearts and our hands to God in heaven and say: "we have sinned and rebelled and you have not forgiven." "You have covered yourself with anger and pursued us; you have slain without pity. You have covered yourself with a cloud so that no prayer can get through. You have made us scum and refuse among the nations." All our enemies have opened their mouths wide against us. "We have suffered terror and pitfalls, ruin and destruction."

Streams of tears flow from my eyes because my people are destroyed. My eyes will flow unceasingly, without relief, until the Lord looks down from heaven and sees. What I see brings grief to my soul because of all the woman of my city. Those who are my enemies without cause hunted me like a bird. They tried to end my life in a pit and threw stones at me; the waters closed over my head, and I thought I was about to perish. I called on your name, lord, from the deaths of the pit. You heard my plea: "do not close your ears to My cry of relief." You came near when I called you, and you said, "do not fear." You, lord, took up my case; you redeemed my life. Lord, you have seen the wrong done to me. Uphold my cause! You have seen the depth of their vengeance, all their plots against me—what my enemies whisper and mutter against me all day long. Look at them! Sitting or standing, they mock me in their songs. Pay them back what they deserve, Lord, for what their hands have done. Put a veil over their hearts, and may your curse be on them! Pursue them in anger and destroy them from under the heavens of the Lord. (Lam. 3:1–66)

These were the cries and plea of Satan himself as he begged the Lord himself to spare his life through prayers. For Satan too had taken form like mankind, in the same way that God did when he made Mary to be of child with the one we all came to know as Jesus. Our Father being the forgiving and merciful person that he is granted Satan's prayer. But only after so much time of affliction and oppression bestowed upon him.

Chapter 19

Whoever remains stiff-necked after many rebukes will suddenly be destroyed without remedy. When the righteous thrive, the people rejoice, when the wicked rule, the people groan. A man who loves wisdom brings joy to his father, but a companion of prostitutes squanders his wealth. By Justice, a king gives a country stability, but those who are greedy for bribes tear it down. Those who flatter their neighbors are spreading nets for their feet. Evil doers are snared by their own sin, but the righteous shout for joy and are glad. The righteous care about Justice for the poor, but the wicked have no such concern. Mockers stir up a city, but the wise turn away anger. If a wise person goes to court with a fool, the fool rages and scoffs, and there is no peace. The bloodthirsty hate a person of integrity and seek to kill the upright. Fools give full vent to their rage, but the wise bring calm in the end. If a ruler listens to lies, all his officials become wicked. The poor and the oppressor have this in common: the Lord gives sight to the eyes of both. If a king judges the poor with fairness, his throne will be established forever. A rod and a reprimand impart wisdom, but a child left undisciplined disgraces its mother. When the wicked thrive, so does sin, but the righteous will see their downfall. Discipline your children, and they will give you peace; they will bring you delights you desire. Where there is no revelation, people cast off restraint; but blessed is the one who heeds wisdom's instruction. Servants cannot be corrected by mere words; though they understand, they will not respond. Do you see someone who speaks in haste? There is more hope for a fool than for them. A servant pampered from youth will turn out to be insolent. An angry person stirs up conflict, and a hot tempered person commits many sins. Pride brings a person low, but the lowly and spirit gain honor. The accomplices of thieves are their own enemies; they are put under oath and dare not testify. Fear of man will prove to be a snare, but whoever trusts in the Lord is kept safe. Many seek an audience with a ruler, but it is from the Lord that one gets justice. The righteous detest the honest; the wicked detest the upright. (Prov. 29:1–27)

"Hello, my son," his dream began as before.

"Papa, what's going on with me?" Mada questioned his father.

"Fear nothing, Mada, for you are perfectly fine, my son. But the time is nearing for the end to come—you must solve the mystery about the girl before it is too late," his father spoke to him.

"How, Papa, how? I don't even know what girl you are speaking of. That alone is a mystery to me, Papa," Mada answered to his father.

"You do know, Mada, and you have help now. But you must hurry, for the enemy grows stronger every day. I love you, my angel," his father said before the demonic figure came and engulfed him in flames.

"I love you too, Papa. I love you too," Mada woke up repeating as the rays of the sun were gleaming through his bedroom window right into his face. There were no cold sweats, no trembling, and no darkness this time, though.

Realizing this, Mada looked at his phone to see what time it was. It read eight forty-five, and he couldn't believe that he had slept in so late after having the dream that would always leave him in a panic. He also couldn't believe that the dream went on for so long. As he placed the phone back onto the nightstand, it dinged, notifying him of a text.

"Federal holiday today, shop is closed, and I'm all yours for the taking if you could stand to be around me for so long," it read from Venus.

"Awesome news, I'll take you up on the offer," he replied back before going to brush his teeth.

"So what can we do with all this extra free time that we have, handsome?" Venus asked him as they sat at the dining room table.

"Whatever you'd like, Vee. I'll leave it up to you to decide." Being able to choose what to do, she thought for a minute before figuring out what she'd like.

"Can we go to the beach?" she asked, seeking his opinion on her suggestion.

"Of course, we can. The beach is never a bad idea, and I have some shorts and a towel already in my gym bag," he said.

"*Yay*," she screamed playfully, jumping up and down and also clapping her hands together like a little kid. "I just need a few minutes to find my bathing suit and pack a bag."

Not wanting to have to worry about having to haul a big cooler around, they decided to go to the inlet, which also happened to have a restaurant and a small bait shop which sold snacks and drinks too. The weather was perfect as the day was still young, and it was bound to warm up even more by midafternoon. Mada told her everything about his dream and how it had played out differently this time. He also told her about his conversation with the reverend from the night before when he was given a ride back to his car and how the reverend asked for him to join up on the podium to give a speech.

"What? You're kidding, right? You? Pastor DeSol," Venus said jokingly to him.

"Come to think about it, the name has a kind of catchy ring to it." She repeated it, but only this time in her native tongue of Spanish, making it rhyme even more this time. "Pastor DeSol." She broke out into a fit of laughter.

They were having an amazing time together in the inlet. They swam, saw some dolphins nearby, and were even fortunate enough to literally stumble upon one of the many manatees which happened to call Florida home. It resembled a big stone in the water as it laid still, lazily swimming away among the many people who happened to also be in the waters, only after Mada tripped over its tail and giving it a spook, which at the same time gave him just as much of a fright having been his first time ever seeing one, let alone this close by in radius.

"Can we go get something to eat?" Venus asked, having worked up in appetite from all the fun they were having in the water. They gathered their few belongings and headed up to the bayside restaurant.

"So do you know what you'll be preaching about this Sunday, Pastor?" Venus said as she took a bite out of her burger while at the same time tossing a French fry to one of the seagulls that flew overhead of the table.

"I have not a clue, Vee. I just felt as if I couldn't say no to the reverend," he answered her as he took a bite from his own sandwich. As they sat there trying to digest what was in their mouths, they heard the sounds of "Happy Birthday" getting louder. Upon looking up, they could see the waiters and some other servers bringing out a cake among a small crowd which were a few tables away from theirs. In the center of the crowd was a very elderly woman, and when the waiter neared her with the cake, Mada could see that she was turning a hundred years old by the candles on it. He almost choked on his food as he realized what his father had been trying to tell him, or so he thought, as he recalled the reverend not being able to answer how old Eve was at the time of her death.

"Oh my god, Vee, I got it now," he yelled in exclamation, half scaring her to death as he startled her from his excitement.

"My dream with my father and solving the mystery about the girl—I think that it has to do with the Bible and with Eve," he said, trying to fill her in about it.

"Do you think that the library is open today?" he asked her, not knowing himself because of the holiday.

"I'm not sure, but we can check online," she said, trying to be of help. He pulled out his phone and search for the nearby libraries.

"Bingo," he said, noticing that one of the three happened to be open, but only for limited hours. "Vee, if you don't mind, can we cut things short here for the day? I promise to make it up to you." He wanted to make sure that he could make it to the library in time to do the research that he intended to do.

"I'm fine with that. This sun was starting to take a toll on me anyway," she said, looking at the color which she had gotten in a matter of a few hours. "But if you don't mind, I still like to spend the rest of the day with you and whatever you have in mind."

They finished their food, grabbed their things, and headed to the car, but not before he stopped by the elderly lady, wished her a happy birthday, and told her thank you.

He set his GPS for the library and immediately took off with adrenaline and anticipation running through his veins. He turned on the radio and from the speakers heard the last verse of "Victory in Jesus" playing through the speakers.

"God, if I am right about my assumptions, then this would truly be a victory for you," Mada said, talking to the radio. Venus just looked at him and smiled in admiration at the end of the determination that was now driving him. They arrived to the library with an hour and a half to spare before it was scheduled to close. Neither one of them having a membership card, they had to both request for a guest pass.

"So what am I to do here with you?" Venus asked, wanting to be of the most assistance to him.

"Research on Eve, or anything pertaining to her," Mada said. "Make sure to take notes please." He handed her a pencil and some scrap paper which he had grabbed while they registered for their passes. After about forty minutes of searching, they had only come up with what was spoken about in Genesis and a few other minor mentions throughout some of the other books, but nothing of much merit.

"Let's try the Quran and other religions," he suggested, knowing that there were many comparisons between Christianity and the Muslim religion. Which is why the two have been at war among one another for so long. He remembered his father's death as he made the suggestion and gave it thought. They were only able to add a few more notes from their other searches before being told that their time was up due to the library having to close.

"I'm sorry, Mada. I hope that these few notes help you in some way," Venus said to him as she handed him her piece of paper and saw the look of disappointment across his face.

"It's okay, Vee. Thanks for helping, though," he replied as he shut down the computer and rose to get going. As he stood, he felt one of his dizzy spells coming on which caused him to have to sit back down quickly, Venus's piece of paper falling out of his hand and onto the floor. As he sat there trying to give himself time to feel better, he read the scripture with she had wrote down on her paper from Genesis 3:20–23.

> Adam named his wife Eve, because she would become the mother of all the living. The Lord God made garments of skin for Adam and his wife and clothed them. And the Lord God said, "The man has now become like one of us, knowing good and evil. He must not be allowed to reach out his hand and take also from the tree of Life and eat, and live forever. So the Lord God banished him from the garden of Eden.

He read her handwriting, his head continuing to spin even as he sat. He read it over again, given that his head was still spinning. This time seeing something which stuck out to him.

"Oh my god, Venus Milagros De La Crux," he said, looking at it again and letting it sink into his mind. "Vee, please read verse 22, and what the Lord God said." He reached down for the paper and handed it to her.

95

CHAPTER 20

After Jesus said this, he looked towards heaven and prayed: "Father, the hour has come. Glorify your son, that your son may glorify you. For you granted him authority over all people that he might give eternal life to all those you have given him. Now this is eternal life: that they know you, the only true god, and Jesus Christ, whom you have sent. I have brought you glory on Earth by finishing the work you gave me to do. And now, Father, glorify me in your presence with glory I had with you before the world began. "I have revealed you to those whom you gave me out of the world. They were yours; you gave them to me and they have obeyed your word. Now they know that everything you have given me comes from you. Before I gave them the words you gave me and they accepted them. They knew with certainty that I came from you, and they believed that you sent me. I pray for them. I am not praying for the world, but for those you have given me, for they are yours. All I have is yours, and all you have is mine. And glory has come to me through them. I will remain in the world no longer, but they are still in the world and I am coming to you. Holy Father, protect them by the power of your name, the name you gave me, so that they may be one as we are one. While I was with them, I protected dumb and kept them safe by that name you gave me. None has been lost except the one doomed to destruction so that Scripture would be fulfilled. I am coming to you now, but I say these things will I am still in the world, so that they may have the full measure of my joy within them. I have given them your word and the world has hated them, for they are not of the world anymore than I am of the world. My prayer is not that you take them out of the world that you protect them from the evil one. They are not of the world, even as I am not of it. Sanctify them by the truth: your word is truth. As you sent me into the world, I have sent them into the world. For them I sanctify myself, that they too may be fully sanctified. "My prayer is not for them alone. I pray also for those who will believe in me through their message, that all of them may be one, Father, just as you are in me and I am in you. May they also be in us so that the world may believe that you have sent me. I have given them the glory that you gave me, that they may be one as we are one—I am them and you and me-so that day may be brought to complete unity. Then the world will know that you sent me and have loved them even as you have loved me. "Father, I want those you have given me to be with me where I am, and to see my glory, the glory you have given me because you loved me before the creation of the world. "Righteous Father, though the world does not know you, I know you, and they know that you have sent me. I have made you known to them, and will continue to make you known in order that the love you have for me may be in them and that I myself may be in them. (John 17:1–26)

"What do you think that means, Mada? For in the Bible, it says that Adam lived to be 930 years before he died," Venus said, still not grasping the whole concept of it even though she was the one who wrote it.

"Vee, it says for the man, but what's to say that it wasn't him that got to the tree but Eve instead? Just like it was her who also took the first bite from the tree of knowledge," Mada said, trying to make Venus understand why he was getting to. "And maybe that's why her death was never mentioned. But don't you think that her being the first woman that she would be remembered just as much as Adam?" His question weighed heavy in the air.

"Oh wow, Mada, what if you're right? For it makes a lot of logical sense hearing you say it," she said, grasping the concept and wrapping her head around it.

"This is big, Mada. This could change the whole outlook of the Bible and everything," she said right before the librarian came and told them that they must get going now.

"Okay, yes. Sorry," Mada said, apologizing and putting the pieces of paper into his pocket.

His hands were trembling as they got into the car. "I have to call the reverend and run this by him," he said to Venus as he reached for his phone and made the call, only to get the voice mail. He didn't leave a message but instead decided to call again.

"Come on, Reverend, answer the phone," he said before getting to voice mail once again. "Darn it, do you know where the reverend lives, Vee?" He wanted so badly to share this wild possibility with the reverend who knew more about the Bible than himself, having been a reverend for so long.

"Yeah, I do. I've been there a few times before with Mama. It's not that far from our place, so just go in that direction for now," she said, getting just as excited as Mada now about what could be the news of the century she thought. They neared Wabasso, and she guided him toward the reverend's place. They proceeded to the front door together and rang on the doorbell. They waited a few minutes before Mada knocked on the door.

"Well, we know that he's here because you park beside his car. Maybe he's in the shower or taking a nap," Venus said, trying to stay on a positive note about sharing the news.

"Let me try to give him another call," Mada suggested while simultaneously ringing the doorbell again. They could hear the ringing of the phone from the inside, which told them what they already know about the reverend being home. Still not getting an answer, he called once more, only this time beginning to walk around the house toward the ringing of the reverend's phone while at the same time trying to look through the windows in hopes of seeing the reverend.

As he neared the bend of the house preparing to make the turn around the corner, the phone's voice mail picked up, causing for the ringing to stop. But there was no need for Mada to call again, for this time he could see the phone through a crack in the window blind, as well as seeing the reverend too.

"Venus, call for an ambulance," he yelled over to her as he himself went through his call log history searching for a number that he was also familiar with.

"Hello, Detective Richards, we have an emergency down at the reverend's house," Mada spoke into the phone explaining all that he could see from the crack while also giving the detective the address.

Within a matter of minutes, there were all yours of first responders, an ambulance, a fire truck, and also Detective Richards unmarked car around the reverends house. Some of these people having to park their vehicles in the grass due to the number of people here now. They had to kick in the door being that all the windows were shut and both the front and back doors being secured. They located the reverend in the side room, to which Mada had pointed out to them.

Being told by Detective Richards to wait outside just in case it was a crime scene, Mada and Venus could do nothing but sit on the small bench by the front porch praying and hoping to hear some good news sooner than later. They needed to not be told anything upon seeing the paramedics pushing the stretcher out the door with the white cover over a body.

"Oh my god, Mada," Venus yelled, reaching out toward him for an embrace and beginning to cry uncontrollably.

"I'm so sorry for you guys, but it seems as if the reverend had suffered a mild heart attack while eating and choked to death," the detective told them as he has exited right after the paramedics and the now deceased body of Reverend Bishop McNeilson.

Mada could do nothing more than just put his head down toward the ground, his eyes shut, as he continued to comfort Venus in his arms. They were forced to have to sit and wait until all the vehicles had left in order to be able to leave themselves. The wait being more excruciating to them, both knowing that there would be no one coming out. Finally, they were capable of leaving and knowing that they never return here again. They were about to head toward Dolores's house to break the news to her. Mada took one last look through his rearview mirror to the house of a man who he considered a real true friend, and as he began to turn, he saw the front porch light flicker a few times. He viewed this as a sign from the reverend's soul saying goodbye to them.

"So what do you plan on doing about this upcoming Sunday now?" Venus asked the inevitable question, trying to break the eerie silence that was in the car.

"Honestly, Venus, I don't know. My mind is so messed up right now that I can't even think about what I'm going to do tonight, let alone six days from now. After all, I was supposed to be his guest speaker, an assistant, so to speak—not run the show," Mada said, frustrated at the reality of it all. They got to Dolores's house and told her the ill-fitting news. She took it just as hard as Venus did, knowing that the man who had saved her life so many years ago had now lost his own.

"Why does God allow for things like this to happen to good people?" she asked neither one of them in particular, more so than she was questioning the Creator himself.

"The good suffer sometimes, not due to God himself but because sin and evil roam this world, always on the prowl seeking out a victim," Mada said, trying his best to answer a question that he really didn't have an answer to himself, having had asked that very question regarding his own loved ones. Although it was still quite early in the evening, Mada had decided that he would go home wanting to do some more research through his phone.

"Care for some company?" Venus asked him, not wanting for him to be alone dealing with everything on his own.

"Sure, Vee, that's fine, but I wasn't planning on leaving the house again once I was home," he said, insinuating that he wouldn't bring her back tonight.

"That's fine with me. I never said that I wanted to go anywhere else," Venus replied to his comment before informing her mother that she would be spending the night at Mada's place.

"Okay, sweetie, you go on ahead. I'll be all right here for the night," Dolores said, realizing that this would be the first time ever that Venus would not be sleeping at home.

"Mind if I take a shower to wash off the saltwater and sweat from today," she asked Mada upon getting to his house and wanting to get comfortable.

"Go right ahead, Vee. I want to look up some more things anyways—there are clean towels in the bathroom closet," he told her as he sat down on the couch to roll up a well-needed blunt to help clear his mind some before getting started on his research.

"Umm, it smells good in here. What kind of incent is that?" Venus asked jokingly upon entering into the living room after her shower.

"That's funny. I left you half of it in the ashtray," he told her as he admired her body. She was wearing a midriff tee, which exposed her flat stomach, with a pair of the velour shorts that weren't doing much to cover all her assets.

"Look at this here," Mada told her as he handed his phone to her, telling Venus how he had typed in the words *she* and *her* for the Bible and found so many passages of how women were in conflict with the Lord or being reprimanded, punished, and even rebuked for this or that—that was displeasing to God in his eyes.

> Long ago you broke off your yoke and
> tore off your bonds; you said, "I will not serve

you!" Indeed, on every high heel and under every spreading tree you lay down as a prostitute. (Jer. 2:20)

Fallen is the Virgin Israel never to rise again, deserted in her own land, with no one to lift her up. (Amos 5:2)

"Have you allowed all the women to live?" he asked them. They were the ones who followed Balaam's advice and entice the Israelites to be unfaithful to the Lord in the Peor incident, so that a plague struck the Lord's people. (Num. 32:15–16)

The woman added, "when we burned incense to the Queen of Heaven and poured out drink offerings to her, did not our husbands know that we were making cakes impressed with her image and pouring out drink offerings to her? (Jer. 44:19)

The list continued on and on with verse after verse of sinful and wicked things that the women of past were doing which went against the word of God.

"You would think that they should have been named 'woe-men' instead from all their evil deeds," Mada said, referencing to all the woes which women had caused back then. "Come to think about it, prostitution was one of the first jobs mentioned in the Bible. And if you look at how woman dressed these days, or listen to the lyrics of some of these female singers nowadays, they're encouraging ladies to use their bodies to get what they can from a man." His comment was making Venus herself feel a little uncomfortable for how she was dressed.

"You really might be on to something here, Mada," Venus said to him, getting complete understanding of it all while at the same time reaching for the blanket that was folded up against the sofa and covering herself out of shame.

"It's out there clear as day now, Vee. Just look at technology like the reverend spoke," he said, with the thought of Bishop McNeilson's lifeless body on the stretcher at the mentioning of his name.

"We have TikTok, OnlyFans, cam girls, and many other sites which have women exploiting themselves for a little bit of attention and a few dollars. Having no respect or self-worth for themselves," Mada spoke, becoming a bit agitated at seeing the commonalities of women today in comparison to those of the past in the beginning of times.

"Oh my god, Mada, you are so dead-on about all this," Venus said, listening to him in amazement for how his mind worked and put things together to make the most perfect sense.

"I'm sure that I am not the only one who has perceived these thoughts, Vee, but the world has become so accepting of sexual immorality that many people turn a blind eye to it. This is why one thing that I did approve of, and actually still do, in regard to the Muslim religion is the hijab and garbs which the women adorn themselves with to cover their body."

"I can understand fully why you feel this way, Mada," Venus said as she tightened the blanket around herself even more.

"Would you mind hearing about my wild and crazy dream while I was in that coma-like spell last week after I fainted?" he asked her as he began to roll up another blunt for them.

"Sure, why not? After all, I love how your mind works," she said as she ran her fingers through his curly hair and massage the scalp. "Can I tell you something first, though, before you begin?" She wanted to make a confession because of all this talk about the women's corruption.

"Why, of course you can, Vee. You can tell me anything at any given time without having to ask for my permission," he said.

"All right, thank you for that, and I just wanted you to know that I am still a virgin," she said.

The comment caught him off guard to the point that he spilled some of the weed out from the half-rolled blunt—these not being the words that he was expecting to come out of her mouth.

"With everything that happened to Mama, I told myself a long time ago that I would save myself for marriage," she said, telling him the secret of her own mother once being a prostitute and that this was part of why she had succumbed to her rape. He shook his head up and down being completely understanding of how and why she had made this decision.

"Let me tell you something, Vee. I admire you for that, and I want you to know that I too am a virgin," he said as he lit the blunt. His confession caught her off guard just the same.

"I've been waiting myself, for a woman who is pure and unde-filed," Mada told her, passing the blunt.

CHAPTER 21

A wife of noble character who can find? She is worth far more than rubies. Her husband has full confidence in her and lacks nothing of value. She brings him good, not harm, all the days of her life. She selects wool and flax and works with eager hands. She is like the merchant ships bringing her food from afar. She gets up while it is still night; she provides food for her family and portions for her female servants. She considers a field and buys it; out of her earnings she plants a vineyard. She sets about her work vigorously; her arms are strong for her task. She sees that her trading is profitable, and her lamp does not go out at night. In her hand she holds the distaff and grasp the spindle with her fingers. She opens her arms to the poor and extends her hands to the needy. When it snows, she has no fear for her household; for all of them are clothed in scarlet. She makes coverings for her bed; she is clothed in fine linen and purple. Her husband is respected at the city gate, where he takes his seat among the elders of the land. She makes linen garments and sells them, and supplies the merchants with sashes. She is clothed with strength and dignity; she can laugh at the days to come. She speaks with wisdom, and faithful instruction is on her tongue. She watches over the affairs of her household and does not eat the bread of idleness.

Her children arise and call her blessed; her husband also, and he praises her: "Many women do noble things, but you surpass them all." Charm is deceptive, and beauty is fleeting: but a woman who fears the Lord is to be praised. Honor her for all that her hands have done, and let her works bring her praise at the city gate. (Prov. 31:10–31)

"Now, you must remember that I was knocked out cold for quite a few hours, so this will be a long story," Mada told her as he was preparing to begin. It started with the Great Pyramid of Giza and how the white man had shot the noses off because they did not resemble the noses of Americans," he said. "Then it switched to the segregation era and the slavery of blacks before a passage of the Bible continued to stick out in my mind for some reason. That passage being Genesis 15:12–14, which I researched, and it says this." He pulled up the verses on his phone. "As the sun was setting, Abram fell into a deep sleep, and a thick and dreadful darkness came over him. Then the Lord said to him, 'Know for certain that for 400 years your descendants will be strangers in a country not their own and that they will be enslaved and mistreated there. But I will punish the nation they serve as slaves, and afterward they will come out with great possessions.'

"Does any of that ring a bell to you?" he had asked Venus to see if she was following along so far. She nodded yes, and therefore he continued.

"Now this next bit of information is going to blow your mind. More passages continued to pop out at me in my dream, like Genesis 17:5: 'No longer will you be called Abram; your name will be Abraham, for I have made you a father of many nations.'

"This passage was followed by Luke 3:23–37, which happens to be the genealogy and bloodline of Jesus. Well, guess whose name I happen to come across in verse 34? Abraham," he answered his own question. "Do you know what this means, Vee?"

"Umm, that Abraham and Jesus were related," she answered hesitantly, not wanting to seem lost or confused a bit.

"Yes, you're right, but it gets deeper than that, Vee. If you follow the bloodline in that passage, it goes all the way down to the beginning with Adam and God. But it's more in-depth than that, Vee. Let's go back to the first passage I spoke to you about in Genesis 15:13: for four hundred years, your descendants will be strangers in a country not their own, and they will be enslaved and mistreated there," he said.

"No freaking way, Mada. Do you mean to tell me that Jesus was really black after all?" Venus said, questioning her own evaluation of what he had just told her.

"Exactly, Vee, and I remember my mother always telling me how my father would always say that the white man is the devil. Now seeing it in this fashion, I have to believe that Papa was right."

"Maybe this is why they shot the noses off the pyramids," Venus added, now sitting up at full attention to hear everything that was being told to her.

"You're right, and it also goes beyond that and includes even the Indians as well. The white man wanted to do away with anyone of color. But their sins caught up to them because although they killed the men of these nations, they had kept the women to fornicate with. Well, what typically happens when you mix breeds of black and white complexion, you get brown tone skin," he said. "So their attempts to eradicate the people of color only made a world of multi-skin-tone people since the whites had the least pigment in their blood."

Venus let out a big "*Wow*" as she intently listened.

"Now I'm going to get into the present, and also what I believe is the future part of my visions from last Sunday. Feel free to have me stop if I'm boring you," he said to her.

"No way, are you kidding me? This is playing out like a movie in my mind as I listen to your story, Mada." Her comment made the two of them laugh a little, although this was serious what he was saying.

"For the present, I saw things that are going on in this world now and today as we speak. The women exploiting themselves was one thing. And it's actually what triggered my mind to recall the rest of these things which I am now telling you, Vee. As you might be well aware of, they are trying to do away with the 'In God We Trust' on money while at the same time becoming welcoming to having 'Satanism' as a religious subject in schools nowadays. This is to show that evil is becoming more acceptable in this world while Christianity—and the Word of God—is starting to be detestable because of sin. It's sad to say, but it seems as if good is beginning to lose between the battle of the gods," Mada said. His words pained as he spoke them.

"Oh my god, we can't allow for this to happen," Venus said, the sound of worry in her voice.

"All right, now this is where it seems that I fell down the rabbit hole like Alice on a psychedelic voyage. I started seeing all these rich and well-known people like Bill Gates, the Rothschilds, the Rockefellers, Queen Elizabeth, and even Elon Musk gathered around a table together, laughing among one another as the whole world was in complete chaos. I saw nation fighting nation, which included but not limited to Russia, Korea, China, Iran, and of course, us here in the USA. It was an ugly scene of destruction as each country was trying to play gods among men," he said. "I came to this conclusion as I had seen multiple laboratories for all different things that are going on today. From the creation of viruses, animal testing to make hybrids, or new species if we can call them that.

"The surgeries for transgenders and even something to do with aliens, which is what led to the last and final part of my dream before I woke up and saw you guys standing there," Mada spoke, trying to catch his breath from all the talking that he had been doing.

Sensing that he was becoming dehydrated, Venus got up and grabbed them both a bottle of water from the refrigerator before quickly rushing back to hear what he had to say.

"Finally, I saw darkness for a while, lots of darkness—and I couldn't tell where I was. That was until I saw the world of planet Earth in the distance. Only then did I know that I was on another planet. It was hard to breathe, and then I noticed that people had these weird apparatuses around their faces with tubes feeding into their noses, which I assumed was fresh air," Mada continued. "And like I said, it was dark. There wasn't much light anywhere, but it seemed as if that's how they preferred it to be. Right then, I saw an image that resembled Jesus on the cross. He was weak but was still able to talk to me and said, 'We need light to survive. They are growing stronger.' I did not know what was meant by this until we did our research at the library. Only then did it dawned on me that in the beginning, the world began in darkness until God created the light.

"These people talked about continuing to travel to other planets from the one which we were on. And what caught me off guard was the lack of women around—for these people were all men. That was until I came to a room where there were many floating devices with all kinds of tubes going into them. Only then did I see the woman who all happened to be within these devices, all of them naked, and all of them throughout different stages of pregnancy," Mada said.

"I noticed some women that happened to be within the labor period and I watched. They separated the baby boys from the baby girls. The girls going into smaller floating devices, and that's when it dawned on me that women were being used as slaves only to create men for wars, I assumed. That was the last of things that I saw before my father showed up and congratulated me, saying, 'Good job, Mada. You did it,' and I woke up," he said.

"Wow, talk about crazy. Let's hope that's not how life turns out to be for us," Venus said with a look of fright upon her face now.

"I agree with you, Vee, so we must somehow begin to spread this message," he said.

"Shoot, and also hope that women begin to value themselves a little more," Venus said before asking Mada if it were okay to share the bed with him.

"We can cuddle and keep each other warm," she added before he agreed to her request. That night, they came together as one flesh as they both made passionate love with one another for the first time in their lives before going to sleep.

The next morning, they woke up having no regrets about what had transpired between the two of them and went about the day as usual. Mada took her home first before he dropped her off at her job. Then he proceeded to make the necessary arrangements for the reverend's funeral and viewing before changing the lettering of the church's message board out front, informing everybody that there would still be service on Sunday and also of the reverend's viewing on Saturday.

The next few days had kept him pretty busy as he tried to work on the message that he would try to put together for his role as pastor.

CHAPTER 22

Therefore, I urge you, brothers and sisters, in view of God's mercy, to offer your bodies as a living sacrifice, holy and pleasing to God—this is your true and proper worship. Do not conform to the pattern of this world, but be transformed by the renewing of your mind. Then you will be able to test and approve what God's will is—his good, pleasing and perfect will. (Rom. 12:1–2)

They could not have asked for a better turnout for Reverend McNeilson's viewing. Mada was surprised to see the great number of people who had come out to pay their last respects to a man who had touched the lives of many throughout his great many years of service in the town. He had gotten the opportunity to meet the reverend's family members, including his two sons who had flown in from out of town for this sad day that actually turned out to be more of a celebration as people told some sort of story in regard to Reverend Bishop McNeilson.

He was a man who was more than just a reverend but also considered a friend and family to many. Dolores was one of the last people to pay her respect.

"These are for your wife. May you guys get to dance when you meet again," she said to the man who had saved her life as she placed her golden shoes into his casket. Mada noticed this and was kind of surprised that she had held on to those things for this long of time.

Sunday morning came, and Mada had found himself in a ball of knots as he got dressed. Preparing to now be the main speaker of the church rather than just a guess. He got to the church early so that he may play the role of greeter as he had come accustomed to seeing the reverend do.

As he shook hands with people, he quickly realized that the church was filling up at a rapid pace. This he figured was due to the viewing service from the day before, as well as people wanting to see who the new pastor would be and how well he'd do. This made him even more nervous now than he was while at home. The place had gotten so full that they had to get the folding chairs that were put away in the basement for when they would rent the banquet hall out for weddings, parties, and whatnots.

And even with that, there were still a nice amount of younger people who would have to stand because of the capacity. If the fire marshal was to come, he clearly would have had to ask some of these people to leave, Mada thought, getting a laugh at his own way of thinking. Finally, there were no more hands to shake, and he casually walked his way up to the front of the podium down the center aisle.

"You got this, cornball," Venus had whispered into his ear as she got up to give him a hug before he began.

"Good morning, ladies and gentlemen of the church, and thank you all for coming out today to hear the word of God," he started. "I'd like to take a quick minute to have a moment of silence for the late and also the great Reverend Bishop McNeilson who was laid to rest yesterday for he was called home by our Heavenly Father and Lord.

"My name is Mada Yosef DeSol," he began introducing himself to the people of the church. "My name's translation is 'majestic angel derived from Adam' and 'I am of the sun.' Last week when the reverend had asked me to join him up here in front of you all, I remember telling him that I wouldn't know what to say or even where to start. To which he had told me, don't worry, the Lord will tell you what to say. Well, my people of the church, I tell you that I have been praying internally that he was right. Considering that I had gotten a case of writer's block the past few days, as I tried to jot something down to have to go off this morning," Mada said, making the congregation laugh.

"I tell you that we are in a time where we're having a battle among gods," he began suddenly. "A battle which they have been fighting since the beginning of time, and we mankind have been the soldiers, generals, and chiefs without even knowing it. This battle I tell you, though, did not start with bullets, bombs, or guns, but rather with *angels, demons, and man*, who were put on *earth to versus evil*." He used Adam's and Eve's names as acronyms. To his surprise, he noticed that many of the people of the church had actually caught on to his play of words as they whispered to one another about it.

"I tell you that anyone who is given life is given one to learn as they live on earth. Which is why we as parents must take the time out of our so-called busy lives and learn to teach our children right from wrong at an early age. But also teach them how to live as well and not just throw a smartphone or a tablet into their hands to keep them occupied. I tell you this for in the Bible, Jesus taught mankind about God because he viewed them as his children. In the same way that God viewed Adam and Eve as his own as well. For no matter how good of a teacher we all are, sin, evil, and wickedness still roam among us. But if we can get a head start on that battle, good will always have an advantage and an upper hand."

He continued with the service informing them about his conclusion about God being of color and the battles that we face regarding Satanism. He touched on many subjects but decided to keep his theory about Eve and the "tree of life" for another day.

"I tell you, my people, that together as one, we can *victoriously eradicate evil*," he said before introducing his newly found wife, Venus DeSol, whom he had married just a few days prior in a rushed marriage just so he could introduce her as his other half.

"Now before I end this service, I read you a passage from Revelations so that we can all get a better understanding of the battle which the gods fight through us," he said as he read.

When the lamb opened the fourth seal, I
heard the voice of the fourth living creature say,
"Come!" I looked, and there before me was a pale

horse! Its rider was named Death, and Hades was following close behind him. They were given power over a fourth of the earth to kill by sword, famine and plague, and by the wild beasts of the earth. When he opened the fifth seal, I saw under the altar the souls of those who had been slain because of the word of God and the testimony they had maintained. They called out in a loud voice, "how long, Sovereign Lord, holy and true, until you judge the inhabitants of the earth and avenge our blood?" Then each of them was given a white robe, and they were told to wait a little longer, until the full number of their fellow servants, their brothers and sisters, were killed just as they had been. (Rev. 6:7–11)

"Thank you all for coming out today to the New Voice of God Church. I hope and pray that I did a good job at filling in on the reverend's shoes, and I hope that you all will welcome me as the *new voice* for this church," Pastor DeSol said before finishing the service with one last acronym.

"In order to find *joy* in this world, one must always put *Jesus and others before yourself*. God bless you all," he finished, to which he got his first standing ovation on his first service. The choir came on stage to close things out with "Victory in Jesus."

CHAPTER 23

But now, this is what the Lord says—he who created you, Jacob, he who formed you, Israel: "Do not fear, for I have redeemed you; I have summoned you by hand; you are mine. When you pass through the waters, I will be with you; and when you pass through the rivers, they will not sweep over you. When you walk through the fire, you would not be burned; the flames will not set you a blaze. For I am the Lord your god, the Holy One of Israel, your Savior; I give Egypt for your ransom, Cush and Seba in your stead. Since you are precious and honored in my sight, and because I love you, I will give people in exchange for you, Nations in exchange for your life. Do not be afraid, for I am with You; I will bring your children from the East and gather you from the West. I will say to the north, 'Give them up!', and to the south, 'Do not hold them back' bring my sons from afar and my daughters from the ends of earth—everyone who is called by my name, whom I created for my glory, whom I formed and made." Lead out those who have eyes but are blind, who have ears but are death. All the nations gather together and the people's assemble. Which of their gods foretold this and proclaim to us the former things? Let them bring in their witnesses to prove they were right, so that others may hear and say, "It is true." "You are my witnesses," declares the lord, "and my servant whom I have chosen, so that you may know and believe me and understand that I am he. Before me no God was formed, nor will there be one after me." I, even I, am the lord, and apart from me there is no savior. I have revealed and saved and proclaimed—I, and not some foreign God among you. You are my witnesses," declared the Lord, "that I am God. Yes, and from ancient days I am he. No one can deliver out of my hand. When I act, who can reverse it?"

This is what the Lord says—your redeemer, the holy One of Israel: "for your sake I will send to Babylon and bring down his futures or the Babylonians, in the ships in which they took pride. I am the Lord, your Holy One, Israel's Creator, your King." This is what the Lord says—he who made a way through the sea, a path through the mighty waters, who drew out the chariots and horses, the army and reinforcements together, and they lay there, never to rise again, extinguish, snuffed out like a wick: "forget the former things; do not dwell in the past. See, I am doing a new thing! Now it springs up; do you not perceive it? I am making a way in the wilderness and streams in the wasteland. The wild animals honor me, the Jack was in the house, because I provide water in the wilderness and streams in the wasteland, to give drink to my people, my chosen, the people I formed for myself that they may proclaim my praise. "Yet you have not called on me, Jacob, you have not worried yourself for me, Israel. You have not brought me sheep for burnt offerings, nor honored me with your sacrifices. I have not burdened you with grain offerings nor wearied you with demands for incense.

You have not brought any fragrant calamus for me, or lavished on me the fat of your sacrifices. But you have burdened me with your sins and wearied me with your offenses.

I, even I, and he who blots out your transgressions, for my own sake, and remembers your sins no more. Review the pass for me, let us argue the matter together; state the case for your innocence. Your first father sinned; those I sent to teach you rebelled against me. So I disgraced the dignitaries of your temple; I consigned Jacob to destruction and Israel to scorn. (Isa. 43:1–28)

"But now listen, Jacob, my servant, Israel, whom I have chosen. This is what the Lord says—he who made you, who formed you in the womb, and who will help you: do not be afraid, Jacob, my servant, Jeshurun, whom I have chosen. For I will pour out my spirit on your offspring, and my blessings on your descendants. They will spring up like grass in a metal, like poplar trees by flowing streams. Some will say, 'I belong to the Lord'; others will call themselves by the name of Jacob; still others will write on their hand, "the Lord's," And will take the name of Israel.

"This is what the Lord says—Israel's King and Redeemer, the Lord Almighty: "I am the first and I am the last; apart from me there is no God. Who then is like me? Let him proclaim it. Let him declare and lay out before me what has happened since I established my ancient people, and what is yet to come—yes, Let them foretell what will come. Do not tremble, do not be afraid. Did I not proclaim this and foretell it long ago? You are my witnesses. Is there any God besides me? No, there is no other Rock; I know not one." Or who make idols or nothing, and the things that treasure are worthless. Those who would speak up for them are blind; they are ignorant, to their own shame. Who shapes a God and casts an idol, which can profit nothing? People who do that will be put to shame; such craftsman are only human beings. Let them all come together and take their stand; there will be brought down to terror and shame. (Isa. 44:1–11)

These are all sayings which the Lord and Heavenly Father had spoken to Isaiah during visions that were to occur during the reins of Uzziah, Jotham, Ahaz, and Hezekiah, kings of Judah. All of which became true to light, for the word of the Creator knew not how to deceive but rather how to hold up rightly and sincere.

CHAPTER 24

In the year that Uzziah died, I saw the lord, high and exalted, seated on a throne; and the train of his robe filled the temple. Above him were seraphim, each with six wings: with two wings they covered their faces, with two they covered their feet, and with two they were flying.

And they were calling to one another:

"Holy, holy, holy if the Lord Almighty; the whole earth is full of his glory." at the sound of their voices the doorposts and thresholds shook and the temple was filled with smoke. "Woe to me!" I cried. "I am ruined! For I am a man of unclean lips, and my eyes have seen the king, the Lord Almighty." Then one of the seraphim flew to me with a live coal in his hand, which he had taken with tongs from the altar. With it he touched my mouth and said, "See, this has touched your lips; your guilt is taken away and your sin is atoned for." Then I heard the voice of the Lord saying, "Whom shall I send? And whom will go for us?" And I said, "Here I am, Send me." He said, "Go and tell this people. (Isa. 6:1–9)

"Hey, Vee, you're up bright and early," Mada said to his newfound wife upon finding her on the sofa in the living room after he had woken up.

"What's wrong," he asked once he noticed the solemn look on her face.

"It had to do with Mama," Venus said in a sad and low-toned voice as she tried to hold back on her tears. "The landlord she was renting from also happened to pass away. His son and daughter have inherited the rights to the deed and have decided that they want nothing to do with the place—and therefore they are planning to put it up for sale now." She informed him of the news where she herself had woken up to when she read the text from Dolores.

"Oh, Vee, I'm so sorry to hear this, my love, but it's not the end of the world," Mada said, trying to console her of her worries.

"You don't understand. Mama doesn't have anywhere else to go, and they're giving her thirty days to vacate the premises. All those years there in that house, all the memories gone now because of greed," she said somewhat angrily because of the hurt that she felt for her mother.

"What do you mean that she has nowhere else to go, Vee? What do you call this?" Mada asked her as he extended his arms out and motioned to the house that they were in. His house, their house, for Venus herself had just relocated with him after their sudden marriage and Dolores telling her that it wouldn't look good in the eyes of the Lord or the people for a husband and wife to live in separate homes, especially not the wife of the newfound pastor of the church which they went to.

"We have two spare bedrooms here, Vee, which she has the choice to choose from. And with all of her belongings, the two of you can now give this place that woman's touch, which you had told me before that was missing here," Mada said as he attempted to be uplifting to her. His comment and gesture caused for a big smile to form across her face.

"You would really allow for her to come here?" Venus asked him somewhat unsure and wanting to get a full confirmation of why she had just heard.

"Of course, my love, I would. After all, she is now my mother-in-law, and the two of you are part of my new family," he said as he took a seat next to her on the couch.

"Oh, Mada, I love you for that, and I also love you for who you are," Venus said as she threw her arms around his neck and gave him the biggest of hugs.

"I love you too," he replied. He registered the exchange of words into his mind, for it had been many years since he had heard or used them, and he hugged her back.

"Also, let her know that she doesn't have to wait until the thirty days are up, and that if she'd like to come now, she could," he added into her ear, as well as informing her that he would rent a hauling truck and help Dolores with the packing and moving since he had the time to do so.

"You know what, you are the best, Mr. DeSol, and I am so thankful that you chose me to be your wife," she said as she planted a kiss on his lips.

"Well, I'm even more thankful that you said yes to my proposal, Vee. Now what's for breakfast, Mrs. DeSol? I'm famished," he said playfully as he excused himself to go wash up quickly.

"So, tell me, Vee, where would you like to go for our honeymoon?" Mada had asked her upon returning from his shower, and he told her to choose from anywhere in the world.

"Oh wow, that's a hard decision that you asked me, for there are so many beautiful places and destinations to choose from," she answered. "But to be honest, I've always wanted to see some snow having lived in Florida forever."

"Okay, very well, my love," Mada said. "I know that at this time of year, besides Alaska or Antarctica, we might be able to see some snow in Colorado," he suggested as he threw out some ideas to her.

"Oh wow, that will be perfect," she shouted with joy in exclamation. "We can kill two birds with one stone out there, for marijuana is recreational, and their prices out there are way lower than ours here." She knew about this because the merchandise and supplies she would order for the "joint" dispensary happened to be ordered from Colorado suppliers.

"Okay, okay, you don't have to twist my arm about it. I'm on board with you," he said, seeing that she made her decision much quicker than he had expected her to do.

"If you'd like, I could look up some tickets and we could go this week from Wednesday to Saturday," Mada suggested to her, not wanting to miss out on Sunday service. Within himself, he was beginning to believe the words of the late Reverend Bishop McNeilson and that the great God Almighty did indeed lead him here to Florida with a purpose.

"Are you being serious right now? That would be great, but what about my job?" she asked, knowing that she could not leave the dispensary clothes for that many days. People would be highly upset if they couldn't get their medicine to help ease their problems and pains.

"How about we ask your mother to run the shop for those few days?" Mada responded. "You can ask her when you call her to mention about moving in with us."

Venus laughed at his suggestion but decided that she would still run the proposition by Dolores—for the worst that could happen was that she'd say no. They finished their hearty breakfast of bacon, scrambled eggs, toast, and grits. Then they headed out to Dolores's house, for Venus figured that she would have more leverage with her proposal if she questioned her mother in person rather than over the phone.

"Oh, why, I'd be delighted to help you out baby girl, especially so that the two of you may enjoy yourselves with some alone time away from here," Dolores said excitedly and without any hesitation upon hearing the requests from Venus. Her response and actions caught her daughter completely off guard, for Venus had expected some type of resistance.

"I could use some getting out of this place myself and enjoying what life I have left on this earth," Dolores said, mentioning about how death had claimed so many lives around her recently and left her with a new viewpoint about life. Her comment left Venus in awe, which caused her to give Mada a dumbfound look on her face.

"What can I say, the Lord works in mysterious ways," he said, shrugging his shoulders up in an "I don't know" fashion as he extended his hands out with palms up. Dolores decided that she would go with Venus to the "joint" for the next couple of days so that she may learn the ropes of the place before they took off for their vacation. Mada gave them a ride to work and also stayed with them himself for an hour or so before heading back home to search for flights, book the tickets, find a hotel and a car, and begin to pack for the sporadic trip. It was about two in the afternoon when he finished with everything and decided that he would lay down for a nap before he would head out to pick up the ladies.

"Hello, Mada, that was a very impressive way to start off as a new voice for the church of God," the voice spoke to him before he could make out whom it was.

"Reverend?"

"Yes, son, and look whom I've run into," Bishop McNeilson spoke again to him in his dream.

"Hello, my majestic angel, I am very proud of what you are doing and whom you are becoming," Yosef said to his son.

"Papa? What is this, you and the Reverend together?" he questioned his father and what was a fresh vision that he had never had before.

"How can this be? What's going on?" he asked them both in a fearful tone of voice not knowing what was occurring.

"Do not fret, my son, for the powers of the Holy Spirit are strongly among you, and what you are witnessing is the wonders of the Almighty One," his father spoke.

"You are so close to discovering the secrets of the mystery. Now open your eyes so that it may be revealed to you."

"I told you that you were special, Mada. The answer lies in the book," the reverend added before they both disappeared, and he continued in a deep sleep with another one of his wild trippy dreams.

R-r-ring, R-r-ring, he woke up to the sound of his phone going off. "Hello, my love, what's going on?" he questioned Venus upon answering.

"Not much, just beginning to wrap things up around the shop here now, and I didn't hear from you—plus Mama invited us for dinner at her place," she replied to him. Mada looked at his phone to see the time. It did not seem to him as if he had slept so long.

"I'll be on my way soon, Vee, and tell your mother yes to the invitation," he said as he got up, rinsed his face off, and darted out of the house. He now raced the clock so that the ladies wouldn't have to be waiting on him outside of the shop. He literally was pulling into the parking lot as Venus was turning the locks to the door.

"Talk about being punctual. That's what I call perfect timing, Romeo," Dolores said upon noticing him putting the car into park.

"Thanks, Dolores," Mada said as he smiled to his mother-in-law, trying his hardest not to seem befuddled with the weird dream which he was having only about twenty minutes prior.

"How was your first day?" he asked her as he tried to distract his own mind and thoughts.

"It couldn't have been any better than what it was. I got to spend the whole day with my baby girl, I was out of the house, and I even saw some old friends from years ago," Dolores answered him, a sound of joy and happiness coming from her voice. Seeing the difference in her and how optimistic and vibrant she was at the moment made him smile once more as he looked up to the sky and thanked the Lord.

"That's wonderful news, Dolores. I'm glad to hear this. Now allow for me to add to your perfect day," he said as he began to drop the top to the convertible, remembering how she had wanted to let her hair blown with the wind.

"Oh my, you're the best son-in-law a woman could have asked for."

"I tell him the same thing about being a husband," Venus chimed in, also wanting to give praises to the wonderful man who she decided to give herself to.

"Thank you both for flattering me. I just hope that you two feel the same way about me the day that I ever let you down," he said with a smile that caused them all to laugh.

"I don't think that is something in your nature, Mr. DeSol," Venus said as she entered the car and gave him a kiss. With that, they were off to Dolores's house to prepare for a great dinner. They all helped each other around the kitchen as they worked on putting together an amazing meal which was made with the best ingredient of all, love. They sat down at the table to a delicious-looking plate of white rice and beans, with a chicken stew made with potatoes and vegetables drizzled on top of the rice. The smell alone was intoxicating. It was an aroma that allowed for the food to be tasted through the sense of smell.

"If you two don't mind, I like to give grace tonight," Dolores said.

"By all means, go right ahead and do us the honors," Mada said.

"Yeah, Mama, your house, your rules," Venus added, and given that, they gathered hands and bowed their heads.

"Heavenly Father, who art in heaven, thank you for the wonderful day and also for these two amazing people who I have here by my side. Thank you also for the life and the acknowledgment to allow me to know that one should not take for granted our days given here on earth. For nobody knows when those days could be numbered. I pray that you may bless this food which we are about to consume and that it may suit us right. But more so, I pray that you may bless us as a whole, a family, and that you may bless these two beside me as a unit. That they may become a team made of steadfast love, always happy to be among each other, always nurturing one another, and always viewing their other half as their number one. And last but not least, I pray that you allow for them to make me become a proud grandmama, Amen," Dolores said, finishing her prayers in a jokingly manner before they got down to devouring the food which waited on them. As usual, they had a great time together as they ate and talked among each other's company. Dolores mentioned to them that she enjoyed herself so much at the joint that she could see herself continuing to help Venus there, even after their return from vacation as a part-time helper with a permanent position. She even told them about her own little mantra that she had come up with after seeing how Venus had used hers to interact with the customers.

"Thanks for choosing the joint, 'weed' love to get you high on the skies," she said, causing them to laugh at the exchange of words between *weed* and *we'd*. Lastly before they departed for home, she thanked Mada for opening the doors to his place and extending his welcome to her. She informed them that she would wait until they returned from Colorado before she would move in with them and that she would take care of the packing herself while they were gone so that she didn't put such a burden on Mada with all that he'd already done for her. They all hugged and kissed one another good night and went about their ways.

CHAPTER 25

They devoted themselves to the apostles teaching and to fellowship, to the breaking of bread and to prayer. Everyone was filled with all at The many wonders and signs performed by the apostles. All the believers were together and had everything in common. They sold property and possessions to give to anyone who had need. Everyday they continue to meet together in the temple courts. They broke bread in their homes and ate together with glad and sincere hearts, praising God and enjoying the favor of all the people. And the Lord added to their number daily those who were being saved. (Acts 2:42–47)

"Vee, I had another weird dream this afternoon that I want to tell you about," Mada said to his wife as they got situated at home for the night.

"Ooh, goodie, a bedtime story. Should I make us a bag of popcorn?" she playfully kidded with him. For truthfully, she knew that his visions were deep, full of in-depth insight, and also a message behind it, like a riddle that needed to be solved.

"I'm all ears and ready to hear whatever you have to share with me, Mr. DeSol," Venus said as she propped herself onto the couch in a comfortable position and motioned for him to come lay his head on her lap. He did as she requested of him and began to tell her about his dream. He told her about the interaction between his father and the reverend and what all they had said to him before getting to the wild part of it.

"There was a timeline which scrolled back and forth between the years of forever ago and the Neanderthal days to the now and present times of today. As the years went from left to right, I saw the lands of the earth. In the beginning, they were mainly connected, but as the years increase to the right, I could see the lands separating into what are now known as the seven continents. This we know from the history books has actually occurred," he told her.

"So has more of what I am about to say, which is what I find confusing. The timeline continued in the same manner swaying from here to there, but each time I saw something different as it did so. From dinosaurs to the Big Bang. Those images of monkeys evolving into erect standing human beings. I saw the elements, rain, snow, hail, and heat.

"As this went on, the letters BC and AD flashed each time that the years hit the center mark. And of course, the dream has some passages of the Bible like before. Mark 13:5–11 and Ecclesiastes 3:18–20," Mada said to her as he finished telling her of his dream.

"What do you take of this, Vee?" he questioned her, knowing that it was her who had pointed out to him before about the passage from Genesis.

"Well, let's start with the obvious and work our way to the harder things," Venus replied. "We know that the glowing letters mean "Before Christ" and "Anno Domini," so you have to figure out what fell where as the timeline changed." She started to help Mada as best as she could, never knowing if she was being helpful or not.

"I also know that of all the animals that have gone extinct or evolved, mankind is the one who has mutated the quickest," she told him, pointing out how penguins were capable of flight in the past until they weren't in need to fly but rather swim.

"But this adaptation took many, many years in comparison to man," she told him regarding the different shapes and sizes of human skulls, including the most recent discovery of the "dragon man skull" found in China by a pathologist.

"Awesome, Vee, we're off to a good start already. Now let's delve into the good book and see what it reveals in those passages," he said, reaching for the Bible that was on the coffee table.

I also said to myself, "as for humans, God tests them so that they may see that they are like the animals. Surely the fate of human beings is like that of the animals; the same fate awaits them both: as one dies, so dies the other. All have the same breath; humans have no advantage over animals. Everything is meaningless. All go to the same place; all come from dust, and to dust all return. (Eccles. 3:18–20)

Having just told him about animals and their adaptations and then hearing what the passage said left her with a eureka moment.

"I think this has to do with man wanting to play as gods, like you mentioned yourself when you told me about your last vision, Mada."

Hearing the words come out of her mouth and being given the reminder made him jump for joy at the realization that his dreams were messing together. Then he heard the words of his father play in his head once more, "You have help now. You can do it son."

At the sound of this, he quickly turned the pages to the book of Mark.

Jesus said to them: "Watch out that no one deceives you. Many will come in my name, claiming, "I am he," and will deceive many. When you hear of wars and rumors of wars, do not be alarmed. Such things must happen, but the end is still to come. Nation will rise against nation, and Kingdom against kingdom. There will be earthquakes in various places, and famine. These are the beginning of birth pains. "You must be on your guard. You will be handed over to the local councils and flogged in the synagogues on account of me you will stand before governors and Kings as witnesses to them. And the gospel must first be preached to all nations.

> Whenever you are arrested and brought to trial,
> do not worry beforehand about what to say. Just
> say whatever is giving you at the time, but it is
> not you speaking, but the Holy Spirit. (Mark
> 13:5–11)

Mada could do nothing more than drop the Bible into his lap as he read that last verse.

"Shut the front door, that's what you said that the reverend had told you when you started your service last week, Mada," Venus said in astonishment as she heard him read the words to this scripture.

"And the part about the wars and the fighting were also in your other visions too," she added. The hairs on her arms came to full attention like those of a cat.

"This is too crazy. You really are prophet, Mada, and I really need to smoke to calm my nerves right now," Venus said as she tried to make sense of everything, looking at her husband with a little bit of fear as everything fell into play in her mind as she recalled about her father, the library, the reverend, his dizzy spells, and more.

"What now?" she asked him, trying to break the silence between them.

"I think that we smoked this blunt and call it a night for now," he said. For he too had his mind racing at a hundred miles per hour from it all.

"We can fill in the blanks sometime tomorrow, my love," Mada said as he passed the blunt to his wife. They smoked enough to mellow them out and then went to sleep.

"Hello, sunshine, how did you sleep last night?" Venus asked Mada, handing him a cup of coffee as he entered into the kitchen to meet her.

"I actually slept great and feel good, my love. You're up early again," he said to her, seeing that it was only seven thirty on the microwave clock.

"Yeah, I had a lot on my mind from what are you shared with me last night, Mada. I went to sleep thinking about it, I dreamt about it, and I also woke up with it all still on my mind," she told him truthfully.

"I'm sorry, my love. Those weren't my intentions," he said as he caressed on the back of her neck to help relieve some of her tension.

"It's okay, you asked for my help, and as your wife, I will do everything in my power to always be there for you. I just hope that you got the revelation that you were supposed to, Mada, for I've been trying to figure out what the elements had to do with it all," she said to him, picking up on their conversation from last night and trying to finish figuring it all out before she had to go to work.

"Oh, about that dash, I forgot to mention to you that the glaciers had all melted, which had caused major flooding throughout the lands," he told her upon hearing of the elements.

"Oh great, another piece of the puzzle to figure out," Venus said, laughing. "But we'll make sense of it all in due time."

"I sure hope so, Vee, and I pray to God that we do so before it's too late."

"Just continue having faith and do as your father and the reverend said. Keep those eyes opened, and search the Bible. The revelation will come to you when it's meant, just like before," Venus said. "You can even look up about the flood there in Genesis." She tried to be of the utmost help to her husband. "Now if you will excuse me, I'm going to go start packing my suitcase some for our trip tomorrow."

As she exited the kitchen, he followed behind her, stopping in the living room and picking up the Bible to do as she suggested and read about the flood. He quickly found the answer to what he was looking for in Genesis 9:11. "I established my covenant with you: never again will all life be destroyed by the waters of a flood; never again would it be a flood to destroy the Earth," he read out loud for Venus to hear as she was filling her suitcase.

"Umph, okay, so at least we know that we won't need to stock up on rafts and life preservers," Venus said. "But I am sure that it has to do with the part of the elements. You do know that man discovered how to make it rain years ago during the Roswell era, right?" she asked her husband, and she began telling him how they would send dynamite up into the skies to blow up and cause the rains to come. "I'm sure that they have perfected that by now. I have also seen on TV something about how we can make clouds now and also a fake sun. You can look all this up on the Internet." She informed him of things that he had no idea of.

"Wow, Venus, I did not know of these things. Thanks for the revelation."

"Oh my god, I think I know what to do," Mada said, speaking his thoughts out loud as he heard this word now for the third time since he woke up.

"What is it, Mada?" she questioned, wanting to be in the known about it.

"Open your eyes and the answer will be revealed to you. The answer lies in the book, the book of Revelations," Mada spoke, reciting lines from both his father and the reverend, as well as what he felt was the missing link to connect everything together.

"Venus DeSol, I think that we're on to something now, my love, and I thank you from the bottom of my heart for all of the help that you have provided me with," he said as he got up and gave her a big hug while kissing her on the forehead. The gesture left her feeling appreciated and honored as she warmed up inside with love. He decided that he would take his time with the rest of his dream so as not to rush things and possibly miss out on seeing something of importance. He took the ladies to work and then scheduled his day accordingly so that he may stay occupied and busy throughout. He hit the gym up, made a few important phone calls, reserved the hauling truck for Dolores upon their return, and also had time to get in a little bit of relaxation while casting the rod fishing.

CHAPTER 26

One of the seven Angels who has the seven balls came and said to me, "come, I will show you the punishment of the great prostitute, who sits by many waters. With her the kings of the earth committed adultery, and the inhabitants of the earth were intoxicated with the wine of her adulteries." Then the angel carried me away in the spirit into a wilderness. There I saw a woman sitting on a Scarlet beast that was covered with blasphemous names and had seven heads and ten horns. The woman was dressed in purple and scarlet, and was glittering with gold, precious stones and pearls. She held a golden cup in her hand, filled with abominable things and the filth of her adulteries. The name written on her forehead was a mystery: BABYLON THE GREAT—THE MOTHER OF PROSTITUTES AND OF THE ABOMINATION OF THE EARTH. I saw that the woman was drunk with the blood of God's holy people, the blood of those Who bore testimony to Jesus. When I saw her, I was greatly astonished. Then the angel said to me: "why are you so astonished? I will explain to you the mystery of the woman and of the beast she rides, which has the seven heads and ten horns. The beast, which you saw, once was, now is not, and yet will come up out of the abyss and go to its destruction. The inhabitants of the earth whose names have not been written in the book of Life from the creation of the world will be astonished when they see the beast, because it once was, now is not, and yet will come. "This cause for a mind with wisdom.

The seven heads are seven hills on which the woman sits. They are also seven Kings. Five have fallen, one is, the other has not yet come; but when he does come, he must remain for only a little while. The beast who once was, and now is not, is an eighth king. He belongs to the seven and is going to his destruction. "The ten horns you saw are ten Kings who have not yet received a kingdom, but who for one hour will receive authority as kings along with the beasts. They have one purpose and will give their power and authority to the beast. They will wage war against the Lamb, but the Lamb will triumph over them because he is Lord of lords and King of kings—and with him will be his called, chosen and faithful followers."

Then the angel said to me, "the waters you saw, where the prostitute sits, are peoples, multitudes, nations and languages. The beast and the ten horns you saw will hate the prostitute. They will bring her to ruin and leave her naked; they will eat her flesh and burn her with fire. For God has put it into their hearts to accomplish his purpose by agreeing to hand over to the beast their royal authority, until God's words are fulfilled. The woman you saw is a great City that rules over the kings of the Earth."

After this I saw another angel coming down from heaven. He had great authority, and the Earth was illuminated by his splendor. With a mighty voice he shouted: "Fallen! Fallen is Babylon the great!" She has become a dwelling for demons and a haunt for every impure spirit, a haunt for every unclean bird, a haunt for every unclean and detestable animal. For all the nations have drunk the maddening wine of her adulteries. The kings of the earth committed adultery with her, and the merchants of the earth grew rich from her excessive luxuries."

Then I heard another voice from Heaven say: "come out of her, my people, so that you will not share in her sins, so that you will not receive any of her plagues; for her sins are piled up to heaven, and God has remembered her crimes. Give back to her as she has given; pay her back double for what she has done. Pour her a double portion from her own cup. Give her as much torment and grief as the glory and luxury she gave herself. In her heart she boost, 'I sit enthroned as Queen. I am not a widow; I will never mourn.'

Therefore in one day her plagues will overtake her: death, mourning and famine. She will be consumed by fire, for mighty is the Lord God who judges her. (Rev. 17:1–18, 18:1–8)

CHAPTER 27

And do this, understanding the present time: the hour has already come for you to wake up from your slumber, because our salvation is nearer now than when we first believed. The night is nearly over; the day is almost here. So let us put aside the deeds of darkness and put on the armor of light. Let us behave decently, as in daytime, not in carousing and drunkenness, not in sexual immorality and debauchery, not in dissension and jealousy. Rather, clothe yourselves with the Lord Jesus Christ, and do not think about how to gratify the desires of the flesh. (Romans 13:11–14)

"Good morning, Vee. Are you almost ready to head out toward the airport?" Mada asked her, wanting to make sure that they arrived with plenty of time to park his car, take the shuttle, and also get their boarding passes for their flight.

"Yeah, just about done now, I only need a few more minutes," she replied that she added the final touches to her makeup. Mada thought he had filled up with gas the night before, as well as loaded their luggage into the car and even packed a bag of snacks and goodies. They had a smooth ride to the airport for the roads were clear and made it with ample amount of time to do everything that was needed of them.

"Are you excited?" he asked her as they waited at their gate terminal.

"Like a clam and sand, but also a bit nervous because this is my first time on a plane," she answered him.

"Don't you worry, my love, the Lord is with us, and we're going to have a safe flight and also an amazing time," he told her in an assuring voice. Not much later, and they were on the plane preparing to be in the skies and on their way to Colorado. He gave her the window seat so that she could take in the view, for he knew that he wanted to take a nap during the flight. He woke up to the sounds of clapping from the other passengers, which let him know that they had arrived and landed safely. Sometime during the flight, Venus must have gotten tired as well herself, for she too was resting on his shoulder. They picked up the rental car and ventured off toward their hotel in Denver.

"Ooh, let's look at these flyers," Venus said as she noticed the multiple pamphlets in the hotel lobby. She grabbed various ones and decided to look them over in the room with Mada.

"Garden of the Gods, dinosaur ridge, what are the odds of that?" Mada questioned as he scanned through some of the flyers with her.

"That sounds very interesting to me," he told her, informing her that he would really like to see those places considering that they had commonalities to his dream. Venus agreed with him, and immediately they were back in the car and off to their first destination.

"Oh, look at that," Venus said as they happened to pass the football stadium for the Broncos as they got on to the highway. Mada offered to take her there as well if she wanted to see it from the inside before they had to return back home.

"Wow, look at the side of those mountains. They go on forever into the skies," Venus said as they were pulling into the parking lot of the Garden of the Gods."

They did the walkthrough and the exhibit building first before going to see the actual rock formations.

"This is so cool and amazing, also breathtaking," Mada said as he gazed up to what was called the "kissing camels" formation. He was awed by the fact that the rocks did in fact resemble two camels facing one another with their noses touching, forming what looked like a heart in between them that one could see through to the skies.

"I like the 'Twins' and the 'Sphere' a lot," Venus said, inputting the statues which caught her eyes the most. All in total, there were twelve formations throughout the grounds. There were even groups of people who were doing rock climbing and rappelling in certain areas. And they even got to see some wild mountain goats roaming freely, a pair of bobcats, and lots of signs everywhere cautioning people of the risk of rattlesnakes.

"Look all the way out that way, Vee," Mada said to her as they stood on top of a boulder that they climbed to take a picture together.

"Oh my god, that has to be the background to our picture," she said excitedly upon seeing the snowcapped mountains in the distance.

"Thank you for this," she said as she hugged him around the waist and placed her head against his chest.

"You're welcome, my love. Now if you're ready, let's head out to our other destination." The drive through the mountains was so serene and scenic looking, also very curvy so that driving on them would be possible, especially in the wintertime with snow and ice on the roads. They made sure to stop along the way at one of the many dispensaries that were scattered everywhere like gas stations. And they were even shocked to see vending machines that allowed people to grab something on the go like a snack machine. They were both thrilled at seeing how accepting and open people here were with marijuana.

"I can't wait for it to be like this all over the world. Astronauts will see clouds on Earth," Mada said as he passed the pre-rolled cone joint to Venus.

"God is good," he added.

"All the time," Venus continued with this worldly known saying.

"And all the time, God is good," they said together in unison as the GPS informed them that they were reaching their destination. Mada had a quick dizzy spell as he exited the car but figured that it had to do with the elevation which they were at now since it only lasted a few seconds.

"Look at the size of this vertebrae," Venus said as she pointed out the enclosed spinal bone of a T. rex sitting out front near the parking lot.

"That is pretty massive. Just imagine how big it would be fully intact," he agreed with her, taking ahold of her hand and walking up the road that others were walking. There were various dinosaur footprints along the now fenced-off rocks and cliffs, which were marked out with black paint so that they were more visible to the patrons. They walked about a quarter of a mile before the road literally stopped. This they found out later on in the souvenir shop was due to the discovery of the bones and tracks as construction to the road had occurred, calling for the government to cease the construction in order to preserve the site.

"From what the story goes, this is where the dinosaurs were running for refuge as they tried to save their lives from the floods of the big bang," the shopkeeper told them as she recited a line which she probably had to tell every visitor or customer as they browsed the merchandise. Venus squeezed onto his hand as she heard what they were being told and gave Mada a look of bewilderment from the news. He purchased a couple of stuffed dinosaurs for Venus and Dolores, as well as a few other small knickknack gifts and a megalodon shark tooth for himself. With that, they called it a good day and headed back to the hotel to relax for the rest of the evening.

"What do you think of about today, and what are the odds of it all?" she questioned him as she dove into the soft comfort of the bed.

"I think that God let us here to give us a sign or a message regarding my dream to be honest—but I'm still trying to figure it all out."

The rest of their vacation was just as busy and fun-filled. They actually got to see the final preseason game the following day live in person and up close, with Venus being given one of the footballs which was ran in for a touchdown by the running back. Friday they went to the "continental divide," where they were able to see how the lands shifted from flat terrain into the glorious mountain tops that they were now on. And they even hiked up Pikes Peak.

A walk that took them a couple of hours considering that this was one of the highest mountains in Colorado at fourteen thousand-plus feet above sea level. They smoked a blunt at the top as an offering to God and hoped that he would help them with the visions. Then they wrapped their honeymoon off with a trip down to Aspen so that Venus could see the snow in person and not just at a distance. They even attempted to ski and snowboard but only found themselves tumbling down the hilltops more than anything.

"I couldn't have asked for more or anything better than the last few days spent with you," Venus said to Mada as they now waited at the airport to return back to the warmth and sun of Florida.

"I have to agree with you on that, Vee, and I'm glad that I got to do it all with you and that you chose this place for us."

"It wasn't my choice remember, but God's doing," she said, giving him a wink and a kiss.

> The song of God's servant Moses and of the Lamb: "Great and marvelous are your deeds, lord God almighty. Just and true are your ways, king of the Nations. Who will not fear you, lord, and bring glory to your name? For you alone are Holy. All Nations will come and worship before you, for your righteous acts have been revealed."
> (Rev. 15:3–4)

"Thank you, choir, for that beautiful rendition to the song of Moses. You may all be seated. As well as all of you here in the house of the Lord today," Mada said in preparation to begin his second service.

"First and foremost, I would like to welcome you all here to the New Voice of God Church, and thank you for coming. I also thank you for being so welcoming to my wife Venus and me as a new voice for the church. As you can all very well see, we have some, shall I say, different and unusual guests among us here today," Mada said as he pointed out the local news crew, a local radio station, and CNM, the Christian News Ministry.

"I invited them all here myself, for the message which I have today, I wanted to broadcast over the airwaves to as many people as I could, with hopes that it will reach out to different nations in the name of our Heavenly Father, to Almighty Creator, Lord of lords, and King of kings," he said, remembering the verse of Revelations 18:3: "For all the nations have drunk the maddening wine of her adulteries. The kings of the earth committed adultery with her, and the merchants of the earth grew rich from her excessive luxuries."

"But before I continue to proceed with my message, I would like to take a moment of silence for all the innocent people who have fallen as victims to the corrupt wickedness at the hands of evil and sin," he said as the whole congregation and himself bowed their heads for a brief moment to honor the dead.

"Brothers and sisters, and people of the church, last week I spoke about a battle that has been going on among mankind through the spirits," he began abruptly and loudly, his voice echoing through the church as he broke the silence.

"And today, I will continue with that topic but also say that the battle began with a woman. A woman that was two weeks within herself to battle the temptations of evil and sin, a woman that we all know goes by the name of Eve!" Mada shouted into the microphone as he mentioned her name.

"Now let me take a moment and apologize ahead of time before I continue, and also say that if anyone is offended by today's message, feel free to leave at any time. For I won't be offended by it, for I am giving my body to the Lord here and now in order for these words to get out to the masses. But first, allow me to continue with this battle among men that we are all aware of—battles and wars that are going on right now at this very moment as I speak into this microphone.

"Battles that are no longer just happening overseas with nation against nation but are also beginning to happen within our very own homes as the youth of the generations become more vulgar and angry at an early age, Causing for father to go against son and brother against brother like Cain did to Abel," Mada continued his speech as the spirit of God ran through him.

"This being due to the divisions of the lands and the stereotypes of race, color, creed, and even religion. But instead of being divided, we should all learn how to have more diversity among ourselves and become more accepting of others for who they are—not what they look like, practice, or believe. Instead of people being so selfish and self-centered, they should learn how to become more selfless and endearing. Only then what these battles begin to subside and dissipate slowly.

"Now I tell you, my people of the church, that these wars and battles come with a hefty price. For besides just the bloodshed, it leaves many women as widows, while others succumb to the lustful ways of the flesh and temptation. Becoming unfaithful and betraying their husbands while these men are away at war, which then causes wars at home among man and woman, husband and wife. So I asked, who really wins from all of these battles?" Mada asked, looking out to the congregation.

"Yet they say that justice is blind, but I beg to differ, my brothers and sisters. She only plays a blind eye to things of her liking, for if she were truly blind, there wouldn't be so much inequality and unjust treatment in the world. This leads me into the next topic of laws and commandments my people.

"The Creator created ten commandments, and ten commandments only, yet man has invented law after law, again to their likings, to the point that we now have thousands of laws to abide and live by. Laws that are tweaked one way or another depending on who it is pertaining to. If you don't believe me, just look at all of the police brutality which has been coming to light since the invention of the smartphone with a camera, and look at how justice tries to justify the ugly acts of the man who hides behind a badge.

"I tell you here and now, my people of the church, that if the Son of God Jesus Christ were alive and walking among us today, he himself would snatch that blindfold off Lady Justice to cover his own eyes," Mada spoke fervently into the microphone as the church went into an uproar.

"He would not want to see any of the perversions and wickedness of this evil world which we now live in. A world in which a thirteen-year-old girl could lie about her age on a social media site that doesn't run social security numbers for true age verification and allow for her to be gawked at by grown men that are older than her own father, allowing for pedophilia to thrive, and not only in this country but also everywhere and anywhere where a cell phone can now get signal. Making prostitution pretty much legal through access of a phone, which brings me back full circle to my first topic of this sermon and Eve," he said.

"Now I will try to answer a question which was asked to our late and great Reverend McNeilson by sister Clarice before his passing, and I say that I am answering your question on assumption only. For I cannot say that this is factual but merely pure speculation on my behalf as I rattled my brain and eyes doing research and reading the Good Book from front to end with everything in between," Mada said, preparing to drop a bombshell that he feared might start a battle within the very church after he'd speak it.

"Sister Clarice and people of the church, please hear me out, and keep your comments to yourselves until I am done. I ask of you. There is no mention of the passing of Eve or the age at which she died because she hasn't died. Now I know that many of you are surely thinking to yourselves that I have lost my marbles, and this is why I asked for you to keep your comments to yourselves until I give you my explanation to this theory of mine," he said.

"Our Father is the Alpha and the Omega, the beginning and the end. And with that being said, I shall read you all a passage from Genesis and also one from the book of Revelations," he said as he took them from Genesis 3:22 to the seventeenth chapter of Revelations verses 1–7. He had gone through his theory about the possibility that Eve had also partaken of the "tree of life" and explaining how he thought that she might have used her body to provoke the angels that guarded the tree.

"Throughout the Good Book, my brothers and sisters, there are many, many mentioning about prostitution and how cities, empires, and also kings fell victim to the adulterous woman. It also says that of all the sins and evil and detestable things which man can do which are upsetting to God, that sexual immorality and debauchery is the one that the Lord and Heavenly Father detests the most for it is a sin which is committed within the flesh. Which leaves me to ask you all a question before I close out this sermon and end with prayer, why do you think God despises this sin the most?"

With that, he was done, and the church stayed in complete and utter silence unto the choir got up beside Mada and began singing, "Holy, holy, holy is the Lord Almighty, precious and forgiving—Christ our Lord."

"Heavenly Father, I humbly pray to you that if I said anything in the house of the Lord which was not to your liking or offensive, that you may forgive me for my sin as I repent to you here and in front of your congregation of fellow worshipers. But if the words which I spoke were your liking, I pray that you continue to find favor in me so that you may continue to fill me with knowledge and wisdom as you use my body to give me the visions to speak to the inhabitants of this earth with whatever messages you feel that needed to be heard. I pray for all those here and also for all those whom these broadcasts may have reached out to. May they read the full book of Revelations to see that the end is near, and I end this with words of the Great One himself, 'Whoever has ears, let them hear what the spirit says to the churches.' In the name of Jesus Christ of Nazareth, the Son of the Holy One, may the people of the churches say. Amen."

CHAPTER 28

EPILOGUE 1

Then the voice that I heard from haven't spoke to me once more: "Go, take the scroll that lies open in the hand of the Angel who is standing on the sea and on the land." So I went to the angel and asked him to give me the little scroll. He said to me, "Take it and eat it. It will turn your stomach sour, but in your mouth it will be as sweet as honey." I took the little scroll from the Angel's hand and ate it. It tasted the sweetest honey in my mouth, but when I had eaten it, my stomach turns sour. Then I was told, "You must prophecy again about many people's, nations, languages and kings." (Rev. 10:8–11)

"Now before I let you all go for the day, I will read you a passage from the Bible to prove my theory about adultery and prostitution."

Yet she became more and more promiscuous as she recalled the days of her youth, when she was a prostitute in Egypt. There she lusted after her lovers, whose genitals were like those of donkeys and whose admission was like that of horses. So you longed for the lewdness of your

youth, when in Egypt your bosom was caressed
and your young breast fondled. (Ezek. 23:19–21)

Mada read this to his class at the university where he taught theology and was known as Professor DeSol. Then he headed out to the dock pier down by the river to wait on Venus so that they could watch the sunset as they smoked a blunt in honor of the Almighty Creator.

"Papa." He heard and turned to see his wife, along with the newest addition to the DeSol family, Evelyn Grace, Evee for short, and they lived happily ever after with the blessings of the Lord.

CHAPTER 29

EPILOGUE 2

"Look, I am coming soon! My reward is with me, and I will give it to each person according to what they have done. I am the Alpha and the Omega, the first and the last, the beginning and the end. "Blessed are those who wash their robes, that they may have the right to the tree of life and may go through the gates into the city. Outside are the dogs, those who practice magic arts, the sexual immoral, the murderers, the idolaters and everyone who loves and practices falsehood. "I, Jesus, have sent my angel to give you this testimony for the churches. I am the root and The offspring of David, and the Bright Morning Star." The Spirit and the bride say, "Come!" And let the one who hears say, "Come!" Let the one who is thirsty come; and let the one who wishes take the free gift of the water of life. I warn everyone who hears the words of the prophecy of this scroll: if anyone adds anything to them, God will add to that person the plagues described in this scroll. And if anyone takes words away from this scroll of prophecy, o will take away from that person any share in the tree of life and in the Holy City, which are described in this scroll. He who testifies to the things says, "Yes, I am com-

ing soon." Amen. Come, Lord Jesus. The grace
of the Lord Jesus be with God's people. Amen.
(Rev. 22:12–21)

About the Author

Luis Marrero was born in the small town of Ciales, Puerto Rico, before relocating with his mother and brothers to New York and then to Pennsylvania. He was always fascinated by the stories of Christ, the Heavenly Father, and the miracles which were performed by our Savior—miracles which he himself could relate to in times of his own life and upbringing. This led him to seek out the truth about what message the Bible has to say and what could possibly be missing from it due to the rewriting of it by man. He is the father of three boys and prefers to live in solitude and peacefully for the most part of his life nowadays.